Lean Six Sigma for Good: Lessons from the Gemba (Volume 2)

Real-life stories and experiences written by Lean and Six Sigma volunteers working with not-for-profit organizations

Brion Hurley

© 2020 - 2023 Brion Hurley

Contents

Introduction 1

Joe Wojniak and Lynn McCullough: Improving Thrift
    Shop Donations 2

Tim Turner: Helping Others By Following The Toyota Way 14

Douglas Cooper: Lessons from Liberia - Standard Work
    as the Foundation for Lean Practices 23

Anita Havemann: Reducing Time and Complexity in Non-
    profit Accounting 44

Steve Bell: Simple Framework for Complex Problems . . 52

Elisabeth Swan: Leaning into the Mission of Childcare . . 69

Tracy O'Rourke: Increasing Meals Per Hour with Kitchens
    for Good 83

Joy Mason: Using Six Sigma to Address Racial Equity . . 102

Resources and Next Steps 112

Introduction

As mentioned in Volume 1, I'm coordinating as many process improvement case studies and lessons learned from those who have worked with nonprofits. These book series are intended to help you get closer to volunteering your skills for a worthy cause, or perhaps you could share this book with someone else to get them to volunteer.

I have reached out to numerous practitioners that have done this work, and asked them to write a chapter about their experiences, both good and bad. The proceeds of the book will be donated to the nonprofit of their choice, split evenly among the authors at the time of release.

We will be releasing the book with updates after each chapter is written, and you will receive the new chapters at no additional cost, so purchase early to get the best deal. If you know someone who would like to contribute, please have them contact me.

If you have questions for any of the authors, their contact information is provided within their chapter.

If you would like more examples of Lean and Six Sigma applied to nonprofits, or would like to check out Volume 1, please visit https://LeanSixSigmaforGood.com

Thank you for reading and supporting the nonprofits of the authors!

Brion Hurley is a Lean Six Sigma Master Black Belt at Business Performance Improvement in Saint Louis, Missouri.

Joe Wojniak and Lynn McCullough: Improving Thrift Shop Donations

Have you heard of the "Marie Kondo Effect"? All over the U.S., people are decluttering their living spaces following Marie Kondo's approach to simplification. She tells book readers and TV show watchers to keep possessions that "spark joy" and get rid of the rest. This has sharply increased the number of donations to second-hand stores nationwide.

In 2018, TRU Thrift Shop was experiencing a similar situation. Many generous people in Boulder, Colorado were donating used items. All day, every day. This flood of generosity meant that the TRU Thrift Shop volunteers and employees were spending significant portions of each day sorting and pricing the donated items. It truly was a flood. Sorting and pricing couldn't keep up with the volume of donations being dropped off.

A Flood of Generosity - the Sorting Room Dilemma

So, how do you approach the impossible? We decided to apply Lean and Six Sigma methods to make changes to the donation process.

Getting Started

The first step was to build a process map, specifically a SIPOC (Supplier, Input, Process, Output and Customer) diagram.

Process Map

Supplier	Input	Process	Output	Customer
Donor	Request for donation pick-up	Donations: Prospects, Pick-up, Receiving	Donated Items	Sorting
Donations	Donated Items	Sorting: Toys, Furniture, Sporting Goods, Electronics, Jewelry, Vintage, Art	Item for Sale	Shop Floor
Sorting	Item for Sale	Stocking & Rotating Shelves	Aged Item	Recycling & Donating, Discard Process
Shelf Rotation	Aged Item	Recycling & Donating to Partner Organizations, Discard	Item sorted for Waste Stream	Recycler / Waste Management / Partner Organization
Stocking & Rotating Shelves	Item for Sale	Sales: Shop floor, Internet	Sales($)	Customer (carry out)
Jewelry, Vintage, Art	Item for Sale	Sales: Shop floor, eBay	Sales($)	Shipping to Customer

As with any organization, the large majority of processes play a supporting role. These are shown in blue on the process map. Reading from left to right, there is a supplier that provides an input to a process. That process produces an output that is delivered to the customer (in many cases this is the next process step.) TRU Thrift Shop was responding to the visible need - thrift shop patrons dropping off donations. This had the unintentional effect of having fewer resources available to interact with store customers on the shop floor.

TRU Thrift Shop is a non-profit organization whose revenues support TRU Community Care. TRU Community Care provides many services to the local community, including grief counseling and hospice. Thrift shop sales are important to supporting TRU Community Care's mission of providing needed support to Boulder County residents. It's important to understand that focusing on thrift shop sales supports the greater mission of doing good.

The next step was to brainstorm a list of improvement ideas, but it needed to be supported by data. An ABC Analysis and trend chart of daily sales illustrated what was being sold and what the daily sales totals were.

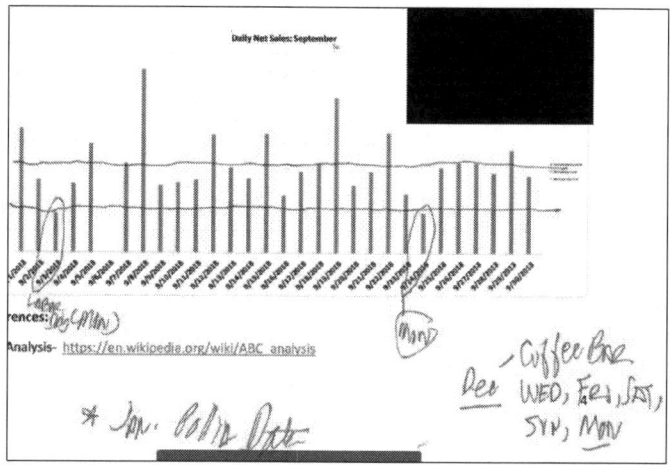

Trend Chart - Daily Sales

The ABC Analysis confirmed some known information, but also highlighted new information. Furniture had long been recognized as a top revenue generating department, which was confirmed, but also that there were several other important departments. For example, Housewares was the second top revenue generating department because of sales volume.

Department	Count	Amount	Inventory Category	Average Amount Per Item
FURN	427		A	
HOUSEWARES	3823		A	
BOUTIQUE	705		A	
DECOR	2136		A	
ACCESS/SHOES	1075		A	
CLOTHING	1308		A	
BOOKS / VIDEO	2680		A	
ELECTRONICS	432		B	
LINENS/RUGS	740		B	

ABC Analysis

After determining the Category A departments, brainstorming could focus on which Donation Room activities supported these departments. For example, a large portion of the Donation Room was being used to store furniture, but this meant that there was less space for the other activities. Furniture would often block the receiving dock doors, which made it difficult to receive donated items, and contributed to donated items being dropped off outside in the front of the shop.

Improvement ideas were collected and new improvement ideas were brainstormed. Lynn collected these ideas from staff, volunteers and she contributed her own ideas. We reviewed these ideas and put them onto an Impact Ease Matrix.

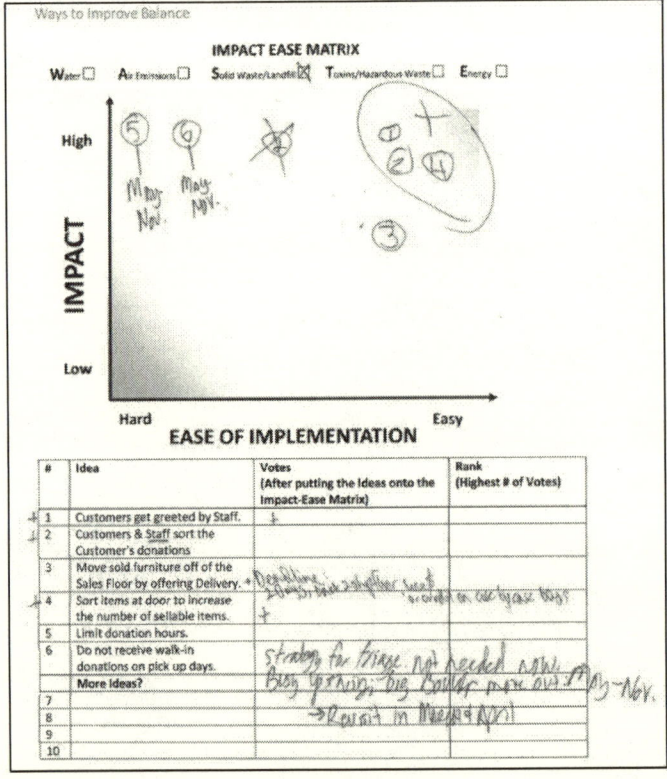

Impact Ease Matrix

The Impact Ease exercise helped prioritize which ideas were important at the moment, while also being easier to implement. This discussion highlighted that there were seasonal changes and that some ideas would become important and need emphasis at different times of the year. For example, ideas #5 and #6 were considered to be more important from May to November vs. February (when we prioritized these project ideas). Ideas #1, #2, and #4 were shown to have the most significant impact vs. the ease of implementation.

The top ideas were:

*#1: Customers get greeted by staff
*#2: Customers and Staff sort the customer's donations together
*#4: Sort items at the door (or at drop-off) to increase sellable items

Sorting items at drop-off meant that customers would keep any unwanted items. This did spin-off a new idea. If a customer absolutely needed to drop-off unwanted items, then the customer could pay a recycling fee to cover the cost of recycling the items.

How do you implement good ideas? You have to convince others that they are worthwhile to implement and that there is a need for change. The staff and volunteers' own experience in the Donation Room confirmed for them that there was a need to change. People didn't necessarily agree on what needed to change, but there was general agreement that change was needed.

The next steps were to have a series of WASTE (Water Air Emissions Solid Waste/Landfill Toxins/Hazardous Waste Energy) Walks in the Donations Room. These are similar to gemba walks, but focused on environmental impacts.

Observations from WASTE Walk

WATER | AIR EMISSIONS | SOLID WASTE/LANDFILL | TOXINS/HAZARDOUS WASTE | ENERGY

Improvement	Kaizen Date(s)	Result
Customers & Staff sort the Customer's donations.	3/15 to 4/13/2019	A Receiving Table has been setup using the space savings in Furniture Donation.
Only sellable items are accepted. - Truck Pick up - Donation Room Drop off	3/15 to 4/13/2019	This is improving with the help of a fee for drop off of items that are in poor condition and cannot be sold.
Limit donation hours. The number of days donations are being accepted are being reduced from 6 days per week to 3 days per week (Friday, Saturday, Sunday.)	3/15/2019 (communicate policy)	Limiting donation hours has made time available to focus on other areas that were falling behind. There has also been space savings in the Donation Room so that donated items picked up by truck have space to be dropped off.
Sell select pieces on Craigslist.	In progress	Items that may sell better on Craigslist have been identified and set aside.

Improvements from WASTE Walk

Some WASTE Walks were used to identify areas to work on. The later WASTE Walks were to focus on specific areas to improve. This was the start of even more improvements to come.

WASTE Walks Results

The dumpster had previously been hauled off 2 days per week with additional unscheduled pick-ups. The rubbish dumpster is now hauled off 3 days a week. This additional pick-up per week avoids the premium cost of unscheduled pick-ups.

Another benefit was the avoidance costs with the increased donations. Previously, all donations were accepted. Roughly 25% of donations are sellable, 75% need to be diverted to other thrift stores, charitable organizations, recycling, and rubbish removal services. If the improvements had not been implemented, 5 dumpster haul-offs per week would have been needed to keep up with the increased donation volume.

- Landfill without WASTE walk and Lean: 5 dumpster haul-offs at $330 per week*
- Landfill with WASTE walk and Lean: 3 dumpster haul-offs at $198 per week*
- Landfill savings: 2 dumpster haul-offs at $132 per week*

*Savings are calculated based upon the monthly average of $793 and 12 haul-offs per month (3 haul-offs per week, $66 per haul-off)

Recycling pick-ups include book totes, mixed plastics and metal recycling. Books that aren't in sellable condition for TRU Thrift Shop are diverted to ThriftBooks and local charitable organizations.

All of these efforts support TRU Thrift Shop's mission to conserve natural resources. It has an existing Zero Waste Program[1] emphasizing recycling, composting, and energy conservation. This program is valued by customers and is one of the reasons that customers shop at the shop.

---

[1] Boulder Colorado Zero Waste, https://bouldercolorado.gov/zero-waste

Volunteers

June is Medtronic's "Project 6" month, a month to volunteer and give back to the community. This supports Medtronic's Mission Tenet 6: To maintain good citizenship as a company.

As a result, a number of volunteers from Medtronic spent an afternoon in the Donations Room sorting items. On a typical day, there might be 1 or 2 volunteers or staff members working in the Donations Room. Medtronic's Project 6 brought 9 to 10 volunteers that could focus on sorting and pricing donations on two separate days in June.

A Medtronic Project 6 Volunteer Group in the Donations Room

An unintended benefit to these focused improvements in the Donations Room is that it encouraged other volunteers to look for ways to improve their areas. As each volunteer area implemented improvements, the indirect social pressure on areas that hadn't improved continued to grow until making improvements has become the accepted norm. Volunteers have been energized and are enthusiastic by being empowered and encouraged to implement improvements.

Why should other Lean and Six Sigma practitioners get involved in nonprofit work?

Lean and Six Sigma practitioners have a unique skill set that can help nonprofit organizations. The same tools and methods that have helped leading companies such as Toyota, Ford, Intel (for Lean[2]) and 3M, Amazon, Dell (for Six Sigma[3]) can also help nonprofit organizations make the most of the talented skills and motivated volunteers that are attracted to the societal benefits that these organizations provide.

TRU Volunteers - Young and...the Young at Heart!

Proceeds

All proceeds from this chapter will be donated to TRU Community Care, Boulder Colorado.

TRU Community Care provides more than $1 million each year in mission-related services for which we are not reimbursed. We rely on contributions from individuals, businesses, and foundations to cover expenses for those with no insurance or means to pay for our services and to close the gap between insurance reimbursement and the actual cost of our care. Our services are funded through various

---

[2]Lean Companies: https://www.manufacturingglobal.com/top-10/top-10-lean-manufacturing-companies-world

[3]Six Sigma Companies: https://en.wikipedia.org/wiki/List_of_Six_Sigma_companies

sources including Medicare, Medicaid, commercial insurance and private payments. All gifts, no matter the size, benefit those in our community—your friends, family, and neighbors—when they need it most. Your generosity makes a TRU difference, right here at home. You can learn more at https://www.trucare.org/truthriftshop/.

Contact

Lynn McCullough

Lynn graduated from the University of Northern Colorado with a Bachelor of Arts in Social and Political Sciences. Lynn has managed the TRU Thrift Shop from the start since 2005. Lynn has guided the Thrift Shop's growth, enabling the Thrift Shop to become a key source of financial support for TRU Community Care's life affirming mission providing hospice services for the community. Lynn has nurtured a fun and friendly environment at the Thrift Shop for customers and volunteers alike. Shopping at the TRU Thrift Shop is fun, economical, conserves natural resources and supports compassionate end-of-life care, grief support, and education in Boulder County, Colorado. Lynn has implemented many earth-friendly initiatives at the Thrift Shop, including Zero Waste which is modeled on nature's waste-free and self-sustaining systems, sharing programs with local non-profit organizations, reuse and recycling that diverts unsellable donations away from landfills.

Thrift Shop Manager at TRU Community Care
LinkedIn: https://www.linkedin.com/in/lynn-mccullough-850a2311

Joe Wojniak

Joe graduated from the Colorado School of Mines with a Bachelor of Science in Electrical Engineering and is currently an M.B.A. candidate in Indiana University's Kelley Direct Program. Joe started his career in Quality in 1999, implementing Statistical Process Control (SPC) and Kaizen improvement at Flextronics-Colorado on 7 Surface Mount Technology and Thru-hole Printed Circuit Board

Assembly lines. Since that time, Joe has held various roles in Quality and Continuous Improvement, including Auditor and Supplier Quality Engineer in the medical device and avionics industries. Joe is a Senior Hardware Design Assurance Engineer at Medtronic in Louisville, Colorado supporting many exciting medical device products and systems.

Earth Belt #1908-001, LRSS™ Black Belt #BB-74511899, ASQ CMQ/OE #54583, CQE #51886
Email: joe.wojniak@gmail.com
LinkedIn: https://www.linkedin.com/in/joe-wojniak/

Tim Turner: Helping Others By Following The Toyota Way

I began my Toyota career in 1995, one week before my 21st birthday. I committed to becoming a student of Toyota. I was blessed with many great mentors during my career. My hope with this chapter is to use some of my previous experiences to inspire you (the reader) to yokoten (sharing) these practices in your workplace and the lives of those around you.

One Team On All Levels

In 2009, Toyota experienced the effects of the economic downturn. Toyota had committed to not lay off any full-time employees from work. They would be put to the test. During this time, I decided to act as a leader and remind all our employees of the great things this company had done for us. Before Toyota came to Kentucky (KY) we were known for coal, horses, tobacco farms, and bourbon. I set out to write a book, called "One Team On All Levels: The Story Of The Toyota Team Members."[4] This would not be a normal book about the Toyota systems, it would be about the people who built the cars at our Georgetown, KY plant. The book would be a collection of testimonies from the workers themselves. We had a story from every level of the company, from the General Manager to the team member building the cars. Over 80 people contributed.

---

[4] One Team On All Levels: The Story Of The Toyota Team Members https://amzn.to/2WCzsd5

The book was far more than just a set of stories. It was a reminder to the leadership that we were all "One Team." We were all pulling together for the greater good of everyone. All the profits from the book were donated to the Toyota Benevolent Fund at Toyota Motor Manufacturing, Kentucky (TMMK). The fund was created to help team members when they experience a hardship.

One example of the fund was from my good friend Brent Pennington. Brent's home burnt down while he was a new hire at TMMK. Toyota gave him money from this fund to help him keep a roof over his family's heads, and helped him with some furniture once he got into his new home. This fund is mainly funded by TMMK's recycling efforts. One way TMMK was able to become zero landfill is by helping the team members see what was in it for them if they followed the proper recycling rules. The Toyota Way in action!

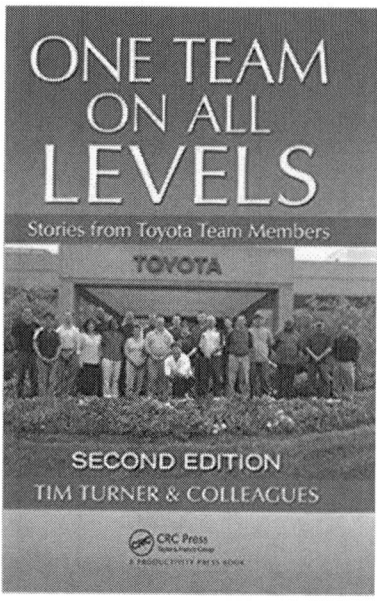

Lex-Pro Partnership

In 2008, I was challenged by then Plant President, Steve St. Angelo, to help a local nonprofit that provided work for people with developmental disabilities. Lex-Pro was a work home for people with developmental disabilities. Much of the work they did prior to 2008 was to package atlases for a large company. Technology slowed down the demand for the atlas, so they began searching for new work. We began the process of finding work for the people through a Toyota partnership.

The project began as a struggle, so we started by creating an A3 to work through the problems. Our first step was to clarify the problem. We determined that the issue was that suppliers guaranteed the parts quality to our factory. No one wanted to drop the parts off to another facility. We had a difficult time finding a part we could take to them. We began to think outside of the box, and decided to bring the team to the Toyota factory. We looked for parts that the team could sub-assemble. We eventually found a part that was being made by a supplier. In 2010, we opted to bring that sub-assembly process into our factory, so that Lex-Pro workers could assemble the rubber bushing onto the exhaust bracket. The process was designed with a poka-yoke. A poka-yoke is a method or device that prevents mistakes. Each workstation was set up with jigs and an arbor press. The team member would place the bushing into a jig, and the exhaust bracket would go onto a hook on the arbor press. The team member would turn the handle on the arbor press until it stopped. This ensured the quality was 100% correct for every part. This type of error proofing is used in all areas of a Toyota plant.[5]

Another issue we had to work around was safety. We wanted to ensure our team would be safe. An automotive factory has a lot of moving parts and equipment, so we strategically found a safe area

---

[5]Toyota leader asks more to provide work for disabled https://www.kentucky.com/news/business/article44075973.html

close to the restrooms and the cafeteria.

In 2012, the Lex-Pro partnership with Toyota was chosen as one of the top 10 most innovative diversity projects in the nation by Diversity Inc Magazine. Dave Orrender (TMMK General Manager) and I had the opportunity to present to two groups about this special team. A lot of companies seemed very interested in helping local nonprofits with a similar-type system. In 2019, policies changed for Lex-Pro's parent company, and the nonprofit had to shut its doors. TMMK gave me the contract, and I hired the same workers, who still come to work every day and complete the work. I'm very proud of this team and all they have accomplished.

In 2011, tragedy struck Japan in the form of a tsunami. One of the Lex-Pro members named Veronica wanted to do something for Japan after Toyota had done so much for them. She asked her other team members to give money. Toyota was matching all donations from team members to donate to the relief efforts. Veronica reached out to me and asked that I make sure the money made it to Toyota. Below is a picture of her presenting the money to a member of the Toyoda family.

Bud Gates Bike Drive

While working at TMMK, I was the chairperson for the Toyota Christian Fellowship Business Partnering Group (BPG). BPG's were a diversity initiative by Toyota to promote diversity and inclusion. We partnered with a local dealership in Richmond, KY to do an outreach event that focused on foster kids[6]. The dealership committed to buying a bicycle for each car sold in the month of May. A group of volunteers came from the plant on a Saturday morning to assemble those bikes in the showroom using Toyota Production System techniques. Our Smooth Motion Kaizen team built an Assembly line, and we built the bikes using a one-piece flow system. The kids came to the dealership and was given the opportunity to ride their bikes off the shipping line. We have done this for 7 years in a row. It's a great opportunity for dealerships to make a difference in the community, and to educate on a simple level how companies assemble products.

Volunteers work on the bike building assembly line

---

[6]Bicycle Building Process for Foster Children Enhanced by Toyota Partnership https://bit.ly/2vDQFYv

TCG Amplify Programs

After I retired from Toyota in 2017, I started my own consulting business, called Triange Consulting Group (TCG). A big part of who I am is to "pay it forward." A division of my business is called "Amplify."

Amplify's goal is to help companies with innovative ideas to make a difference in the world around them, and be good corporate citizens. We set up teams like Lex-Pro in other companies. We help organizations partner with groups of people with intellectual disabilities or homeless shelters. We help organizations choose the right partner organization, and help them set it all up. We even act as a temp agency, to make it easier for their payroll department.

We do a one-week Manufacturing Simulation exercise with companies. We bring in 20 employees and teach TPS basic principles. We take a couple days to build a simple assembly line, and design standard work to build 50 bicycles on Friday. Those bikes are then donated by the company to a local nonprofit organization to give to kids. This is a great way for the customer to gain the value of training, while simultaneously helping the community.

Completed bikes assembled by the manufacturing simulation exercise

The homeless community is a group that needs help. Most are trying to beat some sort of addiction. TCG provides temp agency services for that population. We hire them for 6 months and work with them. The client pays TCG. We pay the worker a portion of their pay and save money for them. Once they have enough money saved for a deposit, we give them that money as a bonus. After they work for us for 6 months and are in an apartment, they can then be hired by any company or a temp agency, and begin the normal process of being a full-time employee. One area where this population often struggles is that they don't manage their paychecks properly, and often fall back into the traps that made them homeless in the first place. Our Amplify program helps them manage through those early struggles as they become a part of the community again.

Proceeds

Proceeds of this book chapter will be given to the nonprofit organization, Center for Quality People and Organizations (CQPO), a joint-effort between the Toyota Motor Corporation and the Scott County (Kentucky) School System.

Their mission is to assist schools in developing students not only as Toyota applicants, but also for college and career readiness. Their program offers teaching techniques for teachers to encourage classroom interaction promoting teamwork and problem-solving skills, regardless of the material or class level being taught.

You can learn more about CQPO at https://www.cqpo.org/

Contact

Tim Turner has spent his entire life surrounded by family. He's been a husband for twenty years, a father for eighteen, and was a member of the Toyota Motor Manufacturing Kentucky family for twenty-two years. While with his Toyota family, Tim held a variety of positions; he was a Fundamental skills trainer for the Lexus ES350 plant, and was the team leader of the Quality Gate and Surface Damage. In its first year of production the TMMK Lexus line won the JD Power Platinum Plant award.

During his time at TMMK, he wrote the book, "One Team On All Levels" with the help of his TMMK family, that focused on various team member's life experiences and how their successes, struggles, and the company developed them as people. All profits from this book were donated to the bereavement fund for the team members at Toyota, who have lost a loved one or experiencing difficult circumstances in life.

He is currently the Family Pastor at Victory Life Church, which allows him to oversee the Care and Outreach Ministries. This has offered him the opportunity to help people from all walks of life in the community. He has begun many programs within the church that help adults and children alike, and show them the love of Christ.

In 2014, Tim was a recipient of the John Maxwell Leadership Award, as one of the top 100 leaders for both his ministry and community commitments. In 2017, he retired to pursue a career in the manufacturing world to broaden his knowledge across multiple businesses. He worked with suppliers, manufacturing sites across 3 locations, and communicated regularly with customers. In 2018, Tim Turner became a John Maxwell Certified Speaker, trainer, and coach. He has used these improvements to mentor and teach teenagers in his community in need of guidance in career and life choices. In August 2019, he started Triangle Consulting Group.

If your organization is interested in any of TCG's programs, or if you have questions for Tim, feel free to send him an email or call.

Phone: 859-489-7425
Email: Tim.turner@trianglecg.com
Website: http://www.trianglecg.com

Douglas Cooper: Lessons from Liberia - Standard Work as the Foundation for Lean Practices

Liberia, one of 54 countries on the continent of Africa, is located about 3 degrees north of the equator, in the lower corner of the great bulge into the Atlantic Ocean that defines West Africa. The country is roughly the size of Ohio, with a population of about 4.5 million citizens, and the 8th lowest gross domestic product (GDP) per capita in the world.[7] From late 2015 to early 2018, I worked in Liberia for Mercy Corps, a large US-based INGO (international non-governmental organization) during the last half of the West African Ebola crisis.

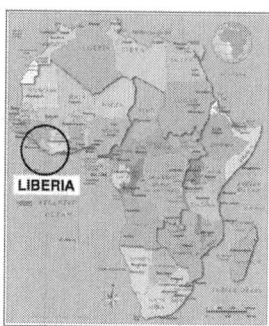

Map of Africa, with Libera highlighted

In late 2017, the country also had national elections and its first

---
[7] GDP per capita
https://www.cia.gov/library/publications/the-world-factbook/fields/211rank.html#LI

peaceful transition of power to a new political party in its history. It was an intense learning experience on many levels, and underlined the value and applicability of lean process management practices even in very chaotic, extreme environments.

The Context of the Work

Liberia is one of two countries on the African continent that was never colonized by a Western or European power. Its modern political boundaries encompass the traditional lands of 15 tribes, with overlapping relationships in Sierra Leone, Guinea, and Cote d'Ivoire. The modern country of Liberia began with the emigration of former slaves from the United States and West Indies sponsored by the American Colonization Society of Philadelphia in the second half of the 19th century. After several decades of limited success, illness and conflict with indigenous tribes, the Congos (as the new inhabitants were called by native peoples) finally gained a toehold in this new environment. Within several decades, they had re-created the social and economic structure of antebellum South with themselves as plantation owners and local tribespeople as laborers. Economic power quickly coalesced in the Americos community and it became synonymous with the Whig political party that held power in the nominally democratic state for nearly a century. In the late 1960s and early 1970s, Liberia was considered a rising star on the African continent. Its economy was beginning to find traction in the emerging international marketplace, primarily by exporting its natural resources of tropical lumber, iron ore and rubber, and its beautiful coastline had become the site of several five star resorts and an increasing tourist trade. That was until a political coup in 1980 and the 13-year civil war that soon followed broke open long repressed social and economic tensions, destroyed the country's infrastructure and fractured its civil life. Liberia has yet to recover.

West African and UN peacekeeping forces intervened and ended the fighting in 2003, and in 2005 Liberia elected Helen Johnson Sirleaf as the continent's first female president. The country began its slow recovery from devastation of the long civil war.

The West African Ebola outbreak, which began in late 2013, added to the country's challenges and reversed the fragile momentum that the country was beginning to build. The virus was first identified in western Guinea and northeastern Liberia. It quickly spread to Sierra Leone, and soon engulfed these three countries in a horrific health crisis that killed over 11,000 people. In August 2014, the World Health Organization (WHO) declared an international public health emergency. Fearing an uncontrollable pandemic, quarantines were established and internal and international trade stopped. Most international flights were curtailed, and the economic growth rate soon went negative, bringing additional hardship, distress and increased poverty to many Liberians.

Although international health agencies were criticized for not engaging effectively in the early stages of the contagion, the international response to Ebola was substantial. Major international and institutional donors like WHO, USAID, The World Bank, the European Union, along with many others, poured resources into the country. In Liberia, the US military built Ebola response hospitals around the country and provided logistical support. There were countless stories of bravery and self-sacrifice as Liberians helped their fellow citizens deal with the terror and effects of the pandemic. By mid 2015, the crisis appeared to be under control, although it was still taking its toll on new victims, and the country's welfare in general. There were also many unintended consequences that accompanied the flood of aid and Ebola relief activities of INGOs engaged in humanitarian response work. Prices and salaries skyrocketed, exacerbating the income inequalities within communities. There was a shortage of experienced Liberian nationals to fill the roles in the many emergency response programs. People with thin qualifications and little experience were often hired and promoted quickly within international organizations to fill gaps in program work. Everyone was doing the best they could in difficult circumstances, but there was an inherent level of chaos that accompanied the massive international response as it encountered the meager infrastructure, lack of local expertise, endemic corruption and a struggling national government. This was the context of the work that I began in the fall of 2015.

Our Programs and Challenges

Mercy Corps had been operating in Liberia since 2002. By late 2015 when I arrived, it was well established as a reliable, effective partner with local communities, civil sector partners and government ministries. The internal organization of our county office in Monrovia, the capital, was typical of an INGO.

The ongoing daily work of our programs and their successful completion relied on the function of three teams:

1. Operations, which managed the procurement of materials and services, logistics of vehicles and drivers and infrastructure of the main office, utilities and communications.
2. Finance, which provided the flow of funds for program activities, oversaw compliance with donor requirements and internal controls, financial management and records and
3. Programs, the staff who were doing the actual work, usually in the communities, that was defined in the grant or contract with the funder. (Overall administration and human resources, while important, supported these teams and their daily work of program implementation).

In 2015, the work of the Liberia country program was proving to be difficult for many reasons. There had been rapid growth in the size and number of active programs, budgets and staff, outpacing administrative and support capacities. There were the stresses of high-pressure, fast paced implementation of emergency response programs, AND the social and emotional disruptions engendered by the Ebola crisis. Our country director had not had the level of administrative support warranted by the size of the expanded program portfolio and level of activity: she was overworked and stretched too thin. There were backlogs in procurement slowing program implementation, and shortages of drivers and vehicles to get staff to the work in the field. Vendors were slow to get paid, and new contracts needed to accomplish program objectives were tortuously slow to negotiate and finalize. Tensions were running high in the organization, and struggles to complete work (while wresting with multiple challenges) often spilled over in frustrations and blame of other teams and leadership. Trust and communications had broken down, and performance at all levels was paying the price.

My initial role as Director of Programs was a new position and was intended to add needed capacity to the senior management team of the Liberia country office. My primary responsibility was to ensure that our programs completed their work successfully, on time and on budget. Because of my past experience with lean process management, I was inclined to see the challenges in front of me through that lens. I had adopted lean process systems as a manufacturing business owner many years before my transition to non-profit work. In my previous position at Mercy Corps Northwest, I had worked with Steve Bell, a lean expert and two-time Shingo prizewinner, and his partner Karen Whitley Bell, who shared my interest in the intersection of lean management and the non-profit world.[8] We had worked together with our US-based Mercy Corps offices on several different projects to extend our learning and adaptation of lean to non-profit work, and in particular, to small-business lending, technical assistance and proposal development. But, these experiences had all been in the U.S., in stable civil and economic systems. This new work environment was extremely different. I was faced with internal and external systems struggling to keep up, a staff that was stressed and on edge, a wall of complex, interrelated issues that were hindering program delivery, in a new

---

[8] Lean4NGO, an organization founded by Steve Bell and Karen Whitey Bell to incorporate Lean principles in support of mission-driven non-profits and NGOs, https://www.lean4ngo.org

culture and unstable environment. I had my hands full.

I want to add a note of explanation and caution at this point: the series of actions, interventions and strategies that are described here did not happen quickly, easily or solely under my direction or management. I was working with and within a team of very dedicated colleagues who all shared the goal of doing our jobs well. When a story is told in retrospect, the necessary simplification and summarization of events can sometimes deceive us into seeing the course of action as cleanly and logically driven, with a sense of predestined success. Nothing could be further from the truth. The processes that are condensed and summarized here were messy, stressful, often shrouded in confusion and moved forward by glimmers of intuition, experimentation and small little learning loops. They did not always move forward in consistent, clear, incremental steps. And while there was an overall logic and direction to the interventions informed by lean management principles, it is only in hindsight that I can see beyond that messiness and identify the key drivers and initiatives that led to substantial improvements. I am convinced that seeing and naming those principles clearly will allow me, and hopefully you, the reader, to apply these tools more quickly and efficiently in future situations. That, of course, is the larger learning loop that moves us forward.

Initial Efforts

Lean management practice teaches that a stable process is a prerequisite to any sustainable improvement efforts, a lesson which Steve Bell had to drill into us several times in our earlier work with Mercy Corps Northwest. In Liberia, we did not have anything approaching a stable system. We were scrambling to complete our tasks and meet our goals and, as an organization, tying ourselves into knots in the process. The volatility and uncertainty of the external environment added to the instability of our operations. My first instinct was to establish some sense of regularity in that part of the environment we could control.

We began with weekly program management meetings. This was a big ask of our veteran program managers who were all much more experienced than me in international program delivery, and who were already stressed and extremely busy. I felt obligated to ensure the time I was asking them to invest was productive. Regular program meetings provided several immediate benefits.

For one, it allowed the program teams, as represented by the program managers, to discuss and understand the common obstacles and frustrations that their staff were experiencing, and which were hindering timely execution of program activities. This began to provide some focus for discussions with the Finance and Operations teams around priorities, blockages and breakdowns in communications. It started the process of identifying and addressing systemic issues that lay at the foundations of the individual complaints and frustrations of each week, and of each program team. We soon added regular meetings with the leads of operations and finance teams. A consistent pattern of communications was helpful immediately, but it was only a first step in aligning our efforts. We were still a long way from root causes, but we were moving in the right direction.

The second benefit of regular meetings was that it provided the opportunity for the program managers to share insights, provide support and ideas to each other. It began to create a subtle but important positive shift in tone, attitude and perception of the challenges we faced. We created a consistent agenda, and began tracking workloads and program status with simple visuals. We recorded short term goals challenges and completions and carried them forward to future meetings for accountability and reference. There is nothing new or innovative about any of this, it is management 101. It did reinforce for me the importance and effectiveness of visualizing issues and problems, making information on status and challenges visible, and shared knowledge as a baseline for common action and understanding.

Stabilization, regularity and consistency became the internal mantra.

The increased sense of predictability began to have a calming effect on the overall zeitgeist of the office. This was reinforced by the resumption of bi-weekly senior leadership meetings (country director, deputy director, program leads, HR, Ops and Finance), regular weekly meetings with my program managers and a regular, monthly all-team meetings for the entire staff.

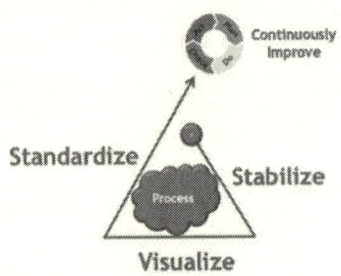

Image courtesy of Lean Enterprise Institute

Our regular weekly "supervision" meetings with program managers were actually more about providing support, prioritizing problems and maintaining a clear understanding of progress on the programs, ongoing tasks and responsibilities. The regularity of standard meetings, with the subsequent opportunities for dialogue, follow-up of ongoing work, and accountability, helped to shift our operational mode from hair-on-fire to predictability. Problems had not been eliminated, blockages still remained, but we were starting to generate a sense of control, cooperation, and stability.

External circumstances were also working in our favor. As the Ebola crisis began to ease in intensity in early 2016, civil life started to recover its natural rhythm. Response programs all over the country were well underway and had settled into established activities with their partner organizations. Ebola vectors and treatments were better understood, and protocols for containing new outbreaks appeared to be successful. There was an increasing sense of looking towards a future rather than being swallowed by an apocalyptic-like reality that had engulfed these three West African nations. These were all positive factors that helped with easing internal tension of the organization, but we still had a long ways to go.

Next Steps

As a country office, we had made some initial progress in identifying key issues that were disrupting program delivery. We were not yet at a point of stable operations that would benefit from regular continuous improvement (kaizen) efforts, but there were glimmers of hope. We had clear standard operating procedures (SOPs) for many of the core functions of the finance and operations teams. These were established agency-wide policies driven by the need for financial accountability, donor compliance and best practices as stewards of our funders' resources.

SOPs, though, can also be problematic. They defined what steps and practices need to be followed, but do not manage how that work flows within the context of daily operations. And while SOPs are an important tool in creating consistency, they can also be used as a cudgel in beating back the demands of colleague teams for quicker, more responsive action. To program staff under pressure and chomping at the bit to get something done, nothing smacks more of frustrating, unresponsive bureaucracy than a deferral to "the finance manual." We chose to take advantage of the structure provided by our SOPs to make improvements in two areas. I will start first with the operations team and the use of instituting standard work with the operations team, our primary focus. I will also touch briefly on work with our finance team that utilized SOPs as a jumping off point for process improvement work.

Confusion of Standard Work vs. Standardized Works

There appears to be some confusion in the lean world around the term "standard work." In some contexts, especially manufacturing or highly process-oriented workplaces, standard work is used synonymously for "standardized work" i.e. a series of highly regular specifications and actions defined for a particular part or step in the manufacturing process. This is certainly a legitimate use of the term, and fits lean's emphasis on eliminating variation that can lead to waste or rework.

The other use of the term "standard work" operates in a the context of understanding work cycles, regular and predictable points of intersection and coordination with other functions in the larger system of production or service delivery. This is also a very appropriate use of the term "standard work." It reflects lean's interest in constructing consistent, efficient workflow across multiple touchpoints in a process or organization, a key tool in eliminating waste in lead times and rework, and in ensuring maximum value for the resources invested in the process. This is the sense of "standard work" which we are using in this discussion.

The image that comes to mind as an analogy of standard work is the inner works of a mechanical clock.

Prim clockwork of a wristwatch, Municipal Museum, Czech Republic. Creative Commons Attribution ShareAlike 3.0 by Kozuch

There are many gears of different sizes, different teeth, stops and ratchets that engage at specific times and planned intervals. All these components must do their part, complete their functions at the right time, in the right sequence in order for the clock to be useful and keep accurate time. Within an organization, standard work defines and organizes those gears and ratchets of tasks, creating a framework for the activities of individuals, the team, and the entire organization. Unlike the gear works of a watch, standard work does not define and determine all the essential activities of a person or team. It only captures the regularly planned tasks and activities which are the necessary skeleton on which everything else is built.

Implementing Standard Work with the Operations Team

The operations team provided logistic support to the program teams and administrative staff, administered procurement of goods and services, and kept the infrastructure of the office and communications systems functional. Breakdowns in any of these responsibilities had negative ripple effects throughout the organization, often compounding into unforeseen problems, re-work, tension and frustration for program teams and administration staff. It was hard to get much done if the electric generators broke down, vehicles were in the shop, teams could not make it into the field, or program supplies were not delivered on time.

A positive characteristic of the Operations team was that they tended to be the most stable, consistently employed staff in the country organization. Programs teams were built and dispersed as grants were won and finished, but the core of the operations team was supported by the aggregation of funding from active grants. It was not unusual to have driver with 5-10 years of service with the agency. This relative stability provided the opportunity to build a strong, functional team that would anchor improvements throughout the country program.

Rollout and Integration

We began the process of stabilization by establishing a clear structure of standard work for the Operations team. We introduced Excel-based standard work templates incrementally, starting with the two senior operations officers, one of whom was my direct report. After an initial orientation to the concepts of standard work and plans for adoption, the first task for of the operations team members was to answer the question "Can you identify your responsibilities that need to happen regularly on cycles of each day, each week, each month or quarter?"

It took several iterations with each team member to create a comprehensive schedule of their respective standard work. Their first inclination was invariably to create a to-do list that encompassed everything that team member felt responsible for, or did in the course of the day or week (usually way too much information). There was also a tendency to reproduce the content of their position descriptions. In both these cases, we had to refocus on the key characteristic of standard work: tasks or responsibilities that were intended to happen on regular, planned cycles. Many of the staff had responsibilities that were mainly responsive to other schedules or demands of the workflow.

The drivers, for example, rarely had two days that ever looked the same. Similarly, procurement officers (for the most part) managed requests from the other teams in the organization, but they had no control over the ebbs and flows of demand. As we identified their standard work, some staff had fewer identified tasks on their lists. It took several conversations to reassure them that their standard work lists, even if they simpler, shorter and less loaded with identified tasks, were not meant to reflect how hard they were working, or how much responsibility they carried. It only identified the parts of their work that happened on a regular schedule. In their case, the bulk of their work was simply irregular. It did not conform to a regular, planned schedule.

The Excel spreadsheet which we created for each team member outlined and defined their standard work schedule (see Figure 1). This was their tool, and their responsibility to print on 11"x14" sheets, and post in their workspace each month. The matrix included checkboxes for each of the tasks which proved to be very useful as a tool for weekly check-in meetings with their supervisors. After each month, the schedule was reviewed, and updates were made as responsibilities were added or changed. I am happy to forward digital copies of the standard work template, simple request via email.

This simple visual management tool is effective for several reasons:

- The initial creation of the list by the team member and his/her supervisor provides the opportunity for clarifying key responsibilities, their frequency, and even the time of execution, if that is critical.
- Regular updating at the end of each month keeps key tasks current and visible. This facilitates coordination with other teams and individuals. It also keeps key tasks from becoming tribal knowledge, which is critical information when people change jobs.
- Identifying and posting the frequency and times of regular meetings with other teams and individuals helps to ensure coordination and execution.
- The list essentially constitutes an agreement and commitment by the team member and his/her supervisor. This provides a baseline of expected performance that is clear, objective and transparent. It is a great tool as a jumping off spot in weekly supervision meetings to discuss workload, obstacles and needed support.
- As new tasks are integrated into regular processes, having your team's standard work visible and readily available helps to ensure the task is assigned, understood and integrated immediately.

- It can be helpful for understanding and making adjustments to a team member's workload.
- Notice that updating, printing and posting the next month's standard work matrix is built into the regular monthly tasks.

Since effective use of this tool relies on consistent application, I had to model this effort with my Operations manager. We met weekly, and reviewed his matrix, discussed challenges and outstanding issues, and made notes and modifications for the next month's iteration. We would then walk over to his direct report, the other senior operations officer who had taken part in the initial rollout, where he would take the lead in reviewing his colleague's matrix. They both learned quickly, and after a month or two, we were ready to roll out the implementation of standard work to the next levels of the operations team.

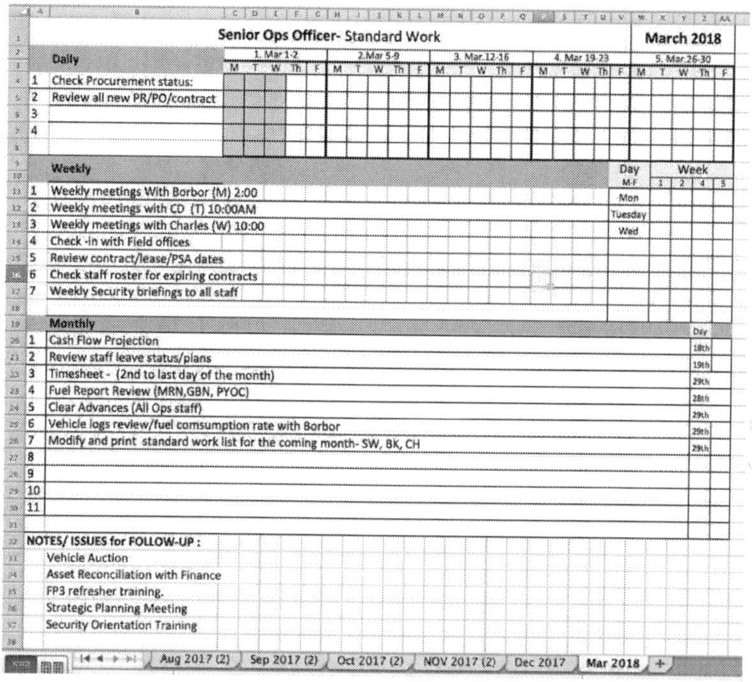

Figure 1. Example of spreadsheet-based Standard Work template

It is easy for misunderstandings and misconceptions to emerge in a new initiative. Consequently, a bit of diligence was required to ensure that the concept, tools and implementation remained true to the standard work model as it cascaded deeper into the staff structure. The best practice of "gemba walks" (being present, asking questions and being engaged where the work is actually happening) is the best remedy for the deviations and misunderstandings that will inevitably happen.

Results

The overall impact of implementing standard work in the operations team was very positive.

- The identification of responsibilities and scheduled work helped to establish a rhythm to the work that promoted a stable, predictable system. This is the necessary precondition before digging in with more intensive process improvement work that we were working towards.
- The implementation of standard work cut down immensely on the inefficiencies the team had been experiencing for a long while. Regularity of oversight, creation and review of performance reports, consistent meetings with other departments, and coordinated schedules all worked together to reduce lead times for key tasks. It also reduced the level of rework of expired or lost documents, inaccurate information, or subverting processes.
- The regular communication and feedback loops that were built-in to all levels of standard work improved communications among team members, and more importantly, with the other departments of the organization. This all resulted in a smoother, more efficient and less stressful system that provided the needed support to the programs team, and by extension, to our participants and stakeholders.

Process Improvement with the Finance Team

In establishing standard work for the operations team, our agency-wide SOPs which defined roles and responsibilities for given tasks gave us a jumping off point for the initial work on process stabilization. Similarly, with the Finance team we used the Field Finance Manual, which define the SOPs for the finance team as our starting point. But in this case, we were able to move directly to improvement work with this team because they already demonstrated a higher level of process stability. Their work and processes were already defined by the Field Finance manual, compliance requirements for funders, general accounting principles and best practices. These multiple levels of agency-wide guidance ensure that country programs meet the requirements of both regular internal and external financial audits. This team, as a functioning unit, demonstrated stability (but not efficiency), making it a prime target for a Kaizen (rapid improvement) event.

One of the consistent frustrations voiced by our program managers was the long wait times to secure reviews and authorizations from the finance team for procurements, checks for vendors, and approvals of contracts. These long wait times often held up direct program activities and operational readiness that supported the field teams. Efforts to accommodate the long wait times by planning farther ahead had not been very successful, primarily because of the highly dynamic, unpredictable context of the field work. Since the required processes were already defined by the Field Finance Manual, we used those process maps to jump start an A3 problem solving analysis. This helped us understand the scope of the problem, explore the root causes, and propose solutions and tracking of results.

We engaged the Finance team in a Kaizen event in which we identified problems and waste in both lead and process times, and distilled down the root causes. We then laid out a new process map, with an emphasis on continuous flow of the documents that needed review, authorization and checks for completion. We set an ambitious goal: any check requests, reviews or authorizations that were submitted by 10:00 am would be approved and ready by 2:00 pm that afternoon. This was a four hour turnaround in a system that typically generated waiting times of a week or more. Success was predicated on having the necessary information and correct forms that came from program staff.

Finance Team participating in kaizen event

This required a parallel effort to engage and educate the Program teams in order to improve the quality of documents they submitted, and eliminate common mistakes, omissions, and resulting re-work.

As we implemented the new process flow, we set up a simple visual management board in the Finance office to record the volume of documents, number of re-works, and average turn around time to complete transactions each day. The board was reviewed with the team weekly, and modifications in the process were made as we encountered unforeseen issues and refined our processes. Over the course of several months, the effort was successful and the "in-by-10, out-by-2" promise was institutionalized and became the norm.

Summary

There is an axiom in the lean world that lean tools cannot be effectively adopted without establishing a culture of continuous process improvement. There are innumerable stories of companies or organizations conducting a one-off "kaizen" event, or an isolated process improvement initiative, without providing a foundation which would sustain their efforts. These short-sighted and opportunistic efforts (which usually die off slowly with questionable results) should be kept in context. They should not incline practitioners to take an "all or nothing" approach to introducing lean practices into a struggling organization. The principles of lean process management, which are based in common sense, scientific process and logic, can be a benefit to any organization.

<u>The key is the order of implementation</u>. Process stability is the baseline, and creates the conditions needed for holistic continuous improvement, step by step. One cannot construct a tall building on mud and expect it to stand, as it will invariably collapse for lack of a solid foundation. The foundation is the first step, and even if progress halts temporarily at that stage, that foundation remains ready for the next step in the construction process. In lean work, stable processes are the foundation from which all other progress proceeds. We found in Mercy Corps Liberia that the adoption of standard work provided an effective, practical tool for establishing a foundation of process stability. We saw first hand the quantifiable improvements that resulted from the process of establishing standard work matrices for the members of the Operations team. We have every reason to believe that the progress we made was sustainable and would continue to benefit the Operations team and the country program, even if no further lean processes were initiated. If there was the opportunity to take the next steps in lean management, the foundation has been established. That is an outcome worth the effort.

Epilogue

I finished my assignment in Liberia before we were able to take those next steps of process improvements with the operations team. This illuminates another inherent challenge in establishing a culture of continuous improvement in development and INGO work. There is often a lot of turnover in both program and senior leadership. In large part, this is because much of the program work is grant driven, with defined time periods for funding and execution. When a program ends, the team is disbanded, and unless there is another program ready to absorb the available staff, they disperse into the community. Often times they end up in employment with other INGOs who are opening new programs and are in need of staff. The opening and closing of new programs directly affects the size of the country program's portfolio, which determines the budget for leadership and administrative staff.

Turnover in leadership and program management complicates efforts to maintain a consistent culture, especially if new leadership is unfamiliar with lean process and continuous improvement work. Some backsliding is inevitable without efforts to review, refresh processes relative to new conditions, and changing contexts. New improvement work consistent with an overall strategic improvement plan can be difficult to prioritize and initiate without consistency in leadership.

These challenges should not prevent us from using lean principles to lay solid foundation that also pay immediate dividends in effectiveness and efficiency. The fact that there will be continuous changes in management does underline the need for creating clear documentation and visual management tools that become integral to daily work. It also points to the need to create a sense of ownership and autonomy of the rationale and logic of processes in the team and its members. This internalization of lean principles (promoting curiosity, experimentation, and learning), can then be carried forward like a positive contagion. It can spread successfully within an organization, and into new organizations, as team members carry their careers forward.

Proceeds

Proceeds of this book chapter will be given to Mercy Corps, which is a global team of humanitarians, working together to alleviate suffering, poverty and oppression by helping people build secure, productive and just communities. In more than 40 countries around the world, their nearly 6,000 team members work side by side with people living through poverty, disaster, violent conflict and the acute impacts of climate change. They're committed to creating global change through local impact, as 85 percent of team members are from the countries where they work. Learn more at https://www.mercycorps.org

Contact

Doug Cooper is an experienced entrepreneur and executive in the private, domestic and international non-profit sectors. Prior to his work in non-profits, Doug owned and managed a design and manufacturing company based in Portland, Oregon for 14 years where he learned and adopted lean manufacturing practices. He has applied lean principles to his work in many different contexts, including organizational development and change management, microlending, asset development, and reentry work. His thirteen-year tenure at Mercy Corps most recently included two and a half years in Liberia as Director of Programs, Deputy Country Director and interim Country Director. He is currently consulting in the non-profit and small business community in Portland OR. His other interests include painting, printmaking, and community service.

Email: dcooper503@gmail.com
LinkedIn: https://www.linkedin.com/in/douglas-cooper-Portland/

Anita Havemann: Reducing Time and Complexity in Nonprofit Accounting

I was once hired for a project to review a nonprofit organization's Accounts Receivable (AR) process, as the Chief Financial Officer (CFO) was increasingly concerned that there was a problem with the AR Specialist worker. The CFO had been receiving numerous customer complaints about mistakes in invoicing. The specialist spoke English as a second language, so the assumption was that the person was the root cause of the AR problems. From my experience, this is rarely the case! I spent a few days shadowing and observing the AR Specialist, taking detailed notes to be able to produce a desk guide. It was very clear to me that the person was not the problem.

The Five Invoicing Systems

There were five disparate customer invoicing systems (for five different service lines of business) and only one of the invoice systems was part of the financial reporting system. One of the systems had a manual process to "upload" most of the data fields into the AR ledger in the financial reporting system, which was the tool used for collections. The invoices from the other four systems were printed and hand-keyed into the financial reporting system. The AR Specialist was also responsible for physically mailing almost all invoices from five different sources to the customers. Only a small percentage were able to be emailed due to having complex spreadsheets to support the invoice.

Here is how the five systems fit together:

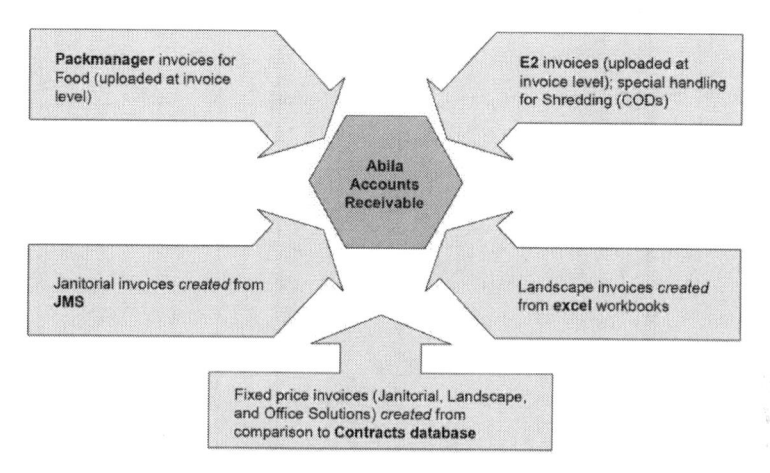

Packmanager invoices for Food (uploaded at invoice level) → Abila Accounts Receivable

E2 invoices (uploaded at invoice level); special handling for Shredding (CODs) → Abila Accounts Receivable

Janitorial invoices *created* from **JMS** → Abila Accounts Receivable

Landscape invoices *created* from **excel** workbooks → Abila Accounts Receivable

Fixed price invoices (Janitorial, Landscape, and Office Solutions) *created* from comparison to **Contracts database** → Abila Accounts Receivable

5 Systems for Recording Invoices in Abila

Thankfully, this organization employed a person who had extensive database programming skills and was Microsoft-certified. Management supported the idea of having them help automate the integration of the customer invoice information into the AR ledger of the financial reporting system.

Turnover and Training New Staff

Meanwhile, the Controller had already taken action to put the AR Specialist onto a Performance Improvement Plan (PIP), which was psychologically crushing to them. From what I observed, this person worked very hard with the tools provided to deliver on the required processes. The AR Specialist started looking for another job, and quickly landed one much closer to home, and with more time to spend with family. This was a huge loss to the organization and probably could have been avoided. To add a little more chaos, the Controller resigned with no notice.

Fortunately, the newly created desk guide became a work in process to train a temporary contractor and later a full-time employee. As processes were improved, the desk guide was updated. A revenue reconciliation process was implemented to ensure the customer invoiced amounts matched the AR subledger amounts in the financial reporting system. Initially, the reconciliation took days, now it is an hour or less per month.

One by one, a process was created to automate (as much as possible) the recording of the invoice details to the AR subledger in the financial reporting system. However, users were able to change invoices in the feeder systems even after recorded in the financial reporting systems, thus making the revenue reconciliation process even more important. A business process was put into place so that when changes in the feeder system needed to be made, the two systems could stay in sync.

People, Processes and Systems

I like this simple way of identifying the root cause because most problems are process problems with some contributing factors from people and systems.

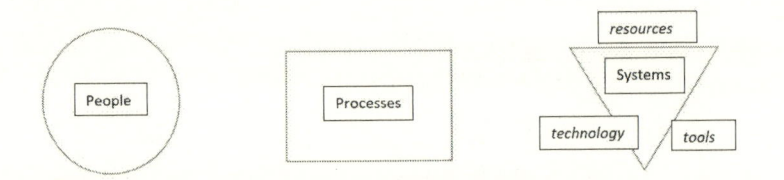

People, Processes and Systems

In this AR process, the main characters (people) did not communicate effectively:

- AR Specialist did not articulate how wasteful the accounting process was (specifically defects, motion, and extra-processing). Why? Perhaps fear of looking like a complainer? Perhaps prior suggestions had fallen on deaf ears, so hopelessness had

set in? Perhaps the person simply could not imagine a better way?
- Controller (and CFO) did not invite the person closest to the problem (AR Specialist) to safely explain the challenges of the job, or job shadow them to seek understanding about these challenges.

Respect for People

In a more respectful work environment, the AR Specialist could feel safe pointing out ways to make the process better, demonstrating employee engagement (vs "complaining"), as long as the management was also willing to explore and implement solutions with the input from all stakeholders.

Managers should remember that if an employee doesn't seem to be a "good fit," they should find out why. Is there a skill gap that can be addressed? Are there tools/resources that are lacking? Is the process sub-optimal? Above all, be respectful. Trust me, when an employee is not performing well, 99.9% of them already know it, so working together to find out why is the humane thing to do. But diving into root cause analysis without first establishing psychological safety will not end well.

For example, when I initially started to shadow the AR Specialist, she looked at me and said, "you're here to take my job!"

I assured her that was not the case, and that the CFO wanted to support her to ensure success. I asked her if she could "wave a magic wand" to fix any aspects of her job, what would she wish? That question helped me establish trust and make sure we addressed her pain points during the project.

Lean Improvements

I also tried to model collaboration with the AR Specialist when I noticed that the Certificates of Destruction from the shredding business were being sent over as half sheets of paper. From that business unit's perspective, they were being cost effective by photocopying two 8.5"x5.5" certificates as one 8.5"x11" copy, and then using a paper cutter to cut into a 8.5"x5.5" certificate for the AR Specialist to keep with the invoice copy.

What they didn't realize is that the AR Specialist was having to place each half sheet certificate on the Multi-Function Device to scan it to a full-size PDF document. By simply walking over to the shredding team and talking about the process with them, they were able to streamline the process by having the shredding team simply feed all of their certificates into the Multi-Function Device to scan and email to the AR Specialist in one fell swoop. What a great Lean win! There are often many opportunities to improve a process by getting two different departments together to talk about the process.

Another opportunity to streamline the distribution of invoices was to survey the customers to determine if they preferred an emailed PDF or a hardcopy sent via mail through the United States Postal Service (USPS). Many actually preferred email, so mailing hardcopies became the exception. This saved the AR Specialist a considerable amount of time (plus saved the organization the cost of paper, ink, envelopes and postage).

Desk Guides

Finally, the responsibilities of the AR Specialist were documented into a comprehensive Desk Guide. The Desk Guide format I used then is different from the format I now prefer – which is a Table of Contents (TOC) that looks something like this:

SAMPLE Desk Guide

Table of Contents
- Heading 1 – Daily Routines 1
- Heading 1 – Weekly Routines 1
- Heading 1 – Monthly Routines 1
- Heading 1 – Annual or Other Routines 1
- Tasks – alpha by name 1
  - Task 1 1
  - Task 2 1
  - Task 3 1
  - Task 4 1
- Troubleshooting – alpha by topic 1
  - Scenario 1 1
  - Scenario 2 1
- References – alpha by topic 1
  - Reference 1 1
  - Reference 2 1

Desk Guide - Table of Contents format

Microsoft Word has a great TOC function that allows the user to go directly to the section from the TOC. Under the Daily, Weekly, Monthly, Annual/Other routines sections, all of the tasks are listed, including context of who/what/where/when. The actual "how to" is listed in the **Task** section alphabetically.

Troubleshooting is a great place to document how to fix mistakes. Every problem is an opportunity to learn how to resolve and document for next time! This ensures the fixes are consistent and saves a lot of time and energy when a new person encounters a problem that already has a documented solution.

Reference Materials is the section to either include or describe where to find items such as company policies, contracts, or any other supporting materials that are needed to do the job.

Desk guides can be another "hot spot" in a work environment that lacks psychological safety. If an employee is told to create a desk guide, they often react with "they're trying to get rid of me."

Instead, the managers should help the employee be engaged in documenting their work processes, and see that it:

- illustrates that the employee has a deep understanding of their responsibilities
- "frees them up" in case other opportunities come along (internally or externally)

With high turnover in many organizations, desk guides are like an insurance policy, shielding them from losing 100% of the institutional knowledge that a departing employee takes with them. Desk guides should be reviewed on a regular basis as processes, software, and references can change frequently.

The strongest teams are those that are engaged and cross-functional. Allow employees to "trade desks" for 30-60 days, and give those desk guides a "test drive"! Train the employees to identify the lean wastes in unemotional terms, since they have a different perspective about this process that they are unfamiliar with. Team collaboration on how these identified wastes can be removed (or at least minimized) is very powerful. As stated earlier, for any of this to work, the environment must be psychologically safe.

Proceeds

Proceeds from my chapter will be donated to Relay Resources, an Oregon nonprofit based in Portland with a mission "to cultivate meaningful work for people with disabilities or other barriers." They have 700 employees and 1,600 affordable housing residents based primarily in the Portland metro area. They provide supply chain solutions (third-party logistics and light manufacturing), building services (janitorial and landscaping) and office solutions (administrative staffing and document services) to local businesses and organizations. Learn more at https://relayresources.org/

Contact

Anita Havemann is owner of Lean Advantage LLC, a process improvement consulting firm in Portland (Oregon) focused on back office and accounting processes. She has completed projects in a variety of industries, and is a volunteer member of Lean Portland (https://www.LeanPortland.com). She holds a bachelor's degree in Finance (Accounting) and a minor in Computer Science from Oregon State University. She passed the Certified Public Accountant (CPA) exam, and has completed several certificates in the Process Improvement curriculum at Portland State University's Center for Executive & Professional Education (CEPE).

Email: leanadvantagellc@gmail.com
Website: https://www.leanadvantagellc.com/
LinkedIn: https://www.linkedin.com/in/anitahavemann/

Steve Bell: Simple Framework for Complex Problems

I'm grateful to Brion Hurley for this new book series, and for asking me to contribute a chapter. As I began to formulate my thoughts, I realized there may never be a greater need for the practices of Lean and Six Sigma to act for the welfare of humanity, and our planet.

We are living in the age of accelerating Volatility, Uncertainty, Complexity, and Ambiguity (VUCA). Our world is made of complex and interdependent systems: environmental, biological, social, cultural, economic, financial, legal, and political. It seems they are all coming to a collective tipping point, and that we must take decisive action on many fronts (consider the United Nations 17 Sustainable Development Goals[9]) to return ourselves to some sort of balance for a sustainable future.

The ability to sort out and focus on priorities in complex systems, taking empirical and measurable action to improve the situation, is what Lean and Six Sigma practices are all about. This action can be taken at the global, regional and national level with large scale nongovernmental organizations (NGO). Action must also be taken at the local level for highly focused issues when put in the hands of smaller nonprofits, motivated communities, microenterprises and individuals.

How is Lean Six Sigma able to support this? Please allow me to offer a very simple framework to think of the principles and practices:

---

[9]United Nations Sustainable Development Goals - 17 Goals to Transform Our World https://www.un.org/sustainabledevelopment/

- Making Work Flow
- Disciplined Problem Solving
- The Learning Organization

Making Work Flow

'Flow' is the core idea in Lean, where work (and the value it delivers to customers) moves quickly and uninterrupted to completion, with high quality, ideally with a sense of rhythm and ease, and outcomes meet the needs of the customer. Think of the last time you felt a state of 'being in the flow' with sports, music, or some other personal activity. This state has been subjected to substantial investigation by neuroscience, and has been studied and reported in depth by Hungarian-American psychiatrist and author Mihaly Csikszentmihalyi, who calls flow "a highly focused mental state conducive to productivity." Individuals, teams and organizations can all experience a sense of flow.

From a workflow perspective, flow looks and feels different depending on the nature of the work that is being done. In manufacturing, production and supply chain operations (where Lean began with Toyota over 70 years ago), it is about the smooth physical flow of production and delivery, with material and labor coming together just-in-time to meet customer demand, with no wasted time, effort, materials or unnecessary cost.

Flow in an office setting follows similar principles, but the work is typically more variable, information-driven and less physical, using mostly paper and data, interactions and transactions, people and complex computer systems, with workflows often spanning large distances, time zones, languages and cultures.

Flow in product design and development also follows the same general principles, but it is focused on the imagination and creation of new products and services, rather than operational excellence in the production and transactions. The world of Agile software development (based on Lean principles) has evolved highly mature techniques to maintain the continuous flow and iteration of ideas through design, development, testing and delivery in all endeavors, not just software development.

In addition to production/operations, product development, and office activities, let's also not forget the flow of information and decision making that is critical to the smooth functioning of management systems in any organization.

Flow in mission-driven non-profits and NGOs can involve all of these types of work: production and supply chain, product design and development, office activity, and management systems. Non-profits and NGOs provide an endless variety of products and services including financial payments and donations, healthcare services, or essential goods like food, water, clothing, and shelter. In the process, they also often develop local capability so each individual and community is better able to improve their own lives going forward.

No matter what work is being done, the flow of the customer journey is critical to understanding how customers engage with you. It is not just in a single transaction, but over the duration of the relationship with your organization (often called the 'customer lifecycle'), to realize not just value, but also a pleasing experience which promotes loyalty and positive recommendations (often measured as the 'net promoter score'[10]).

Often the flow of a process is hidden from view, obscured by the daily stresses, interruptions, chaotic events, and organizational disconnects. The Lean tools of Value Stream Mapping help us "learn to see" the flow by "making the invisible visible." This helps value stream teams understand and measure their performance (end-to-end flow), and identify and prioritize obstacles getting in their way.

The tools and techniques of Value Stream Mapping have evolved considerably since they were first introduced over twenty years

---

[10]Net Promoter Score. Wikipedia https://en.wikipedia.org/wiki/Net_Promoter

ago. Starting in the realm of manufacturing, they have evolved into nearly every industry sector. Initially the Value Stream Map was represented in a circular pattern emphasizing the deliverer's point of view, showing the customer request and receipt as a simple closed loop. The technique later evolved to show two parallel pathways, where the customer journey and experience is overlaid on the delivery workflow, so the team can understand the continuous interactions and transactions that occur between them.

More complex business operating models have emerged over the years, especially with the advent of widespread digitization. A new approach visually represents and measures the various enterprise-wide workflows that must come together across the globe to show a complete value stream. Many digitally proficient enterprises now organize (or re-organize) themselves as value stream centric teams (often called tribes and squads) to concentrate on these specific flows. They must pay special attention to data sources and flows, so the mapping approach must accommodate these new dimensions. These changes have led to a new approach we call Multi-Dimensional Value Stream Mapping (MDVSM) which we hope to publish and share in the near future.

In addition to mapping, there are many other tools and techniques, such as visual management, to help teams see the flow, and quickly spot and respond to problems. One such technique is Kanban, a simple and useful approach to help visualize and manage flow in real time. Kanban was originally developed at Toyota as a way to manage shop floor inventory, and it was later refined by the Agile community as a tool for general project and workflow management. If you visit nearly any software development team, you will see Kanban boards on the walls, filled with sticky notes of various colors, and teams standing by the boards monitoring the flow, clarifying priorities, and identifying problems, to keep the work flowing.

Beyond the specific tools and techniques, the **most** important point is that the team that 'owns' the value stream must "learn to see" the flow so they can monitor, measure and continuously improve it. Value stream mapping and analysis should therefore not be done by an external consulting group and delivered to the team as a finished result – that is very disempowering and tends to produce unsustainable solutions that do not adapt to ongoing changes. The map is a learning device, and the beginning of a continuous improvement effort, not the endpoint. The team uses the map (and associated visuals, measures and feedback loops) to manage the flow going forward, and adapt to change. Value Stream Mapping and analysis must therefore be an energetic, engaged, hands-on, team-based experience (facilitated by a skilled coach) shown in this photo of Grameen Foundation in Kampala, Uganda.

Grameen Foundation team updating a Value Stream Map in Kampala, Uganda

Years ago we engaged in some pro-bono work to help NGO Grameen Foundation scale a successful innovation from Uganda to other developing countries in Africa and around the globe. This innovation involved hiring locals with knowledge of farming and local customs, and equipping them with specially programmed smartphones to visit rural farmers, where they shared information to help these farmers optimize crop yields and sales value. They also provided other knowledge services such as women's and children's health programs. These individuals were called Community

Knowledge Workers. Karen and I were there to help the Grameen Foundation team (based in Kampala, Uganda) transform their heroic, just-make-this-happen Uganda pilot program into scalable, repeatable processes that could be adapted across different cultures and government practices. It was necessary to clearly understand and measure what worked, and determine what could be improved, so it could be effectively scaled elsewhere on the continent, and adapted to unique conditions in each target country. This work was highlighted in a Planet Lean article in 2019.[11]

Once the team that owns the process is able to identify and measure obstacles to flow, they must continuously prioritize and eliminate the obstacles. But intervening in a complex system is never simple, which brings us to the second element, disciplined problem solving.

Disciplined Problem Solving

Lean and Six Sigma emphasize prioritizing and iteratively solving problems in complex systems, to continuously improve, innovate and learn. For an organization to consistently perform under conditions of rapid change, it needs a problem solving mindset and process that can be practiced and repeated consistently across all dimensions of the organization.

By teaching and coaching such a process, a large organization (or collection of organizations working together such as a global NGO working with local partners) can quickly swarm a problem with a group of people that have never worked together before, and immediately be effective.

The steps of such a problem solving process must be simple and logical, but that does not make them easy. Effective problem solving requires the team to slow down and ask the right questions, resisting the urge to jump to 'solutions.' This is important because

---
[11] The path to a learning organization by Steve Bell & Karen Whitley Bell, Planet Lean, June 6, 2019, https://planet-lean.com/lean-visual-management-ngo/

most of what we tend to think of as problems are actually symptoms of underlying root causes. Attacking symptoms may feel good for the moment, but premature 'solutions' that don't consider the underlying root causes usually provide only temporary relief, while making the underlying problems worse.

To be more effective at problem solving, the team must achieve clarity of what the problem is, and why it is important to all concerned. This step helps align all participants on the strategic intent. Next it is essential to define and measure the current condition of what is happening now and the harm that is caused. The team makes observations at the workplace, gathering facts, data, and evidence to create a complete picture that encompasses a variety of points of view.

Problem solving teams should spend the majority of their time on this early phase, since the more they understand the cause-and-effect relationships buried deep within the situation, the clearer view they will have of the actions they must take to correct it, how 'success' should look (the hypothesis), and how they will measure it.

Then they must ask about the long-term goal, to determine what would be the best first step (iteration or experiment) to get there. Sometimes an immediate and radical change is needed to intervene on an imminent and harmful situation. Revolutionary change is known by the Japanese word, Kaikaku.

More often, an incremental change is helpful to stabilize the situation, followed by small improvements going forward. Evolutionary change is known by the Japanese word, Kaizen. With each iteration, the team learns something new and important, which informs the next improvement cycle.

Radical change (Kaikaku) must be followed by Kaizen. All change has a short shelf life, and continuing changes in the environment require the team to continuously improve and innovate. That is why the team must have the knowledge and capability to guide training, visual guidance and process feedback, in order to create consistency in how tasks are performed. Complicated problems are also deterministic but with a far greater need for specialized skills. They are the domain of sophisticated Six Sigma techniques supported by deep data analytic capabilities, and by significant training and often professional development efforts.

Complex and chaotic situations are messier, fluid and fuzzy. These are entirely new situations with no precedents and standards, and are the domain of exploration, discovery, design and development through rapid, iterative experimentation.

It's not only important to understand how to classify the different types of problems, so you can respond to them appropriately. It's also important to understand how problems can evolve. At risk of over-simplifying, most emerging problems (and opportunities) appear at or beyond the edge of what is known, often called the 'fuzzy front end'; unexpected, where disruptive change seems to be a daily occurrence. Adapting to such change can be a full-time job, while we must simultaneously 'keep the wheels on' with continuing operations (whether not-for-profit or for-profit) in order to maintain viability. So there is a continuous cycle of innovation and adaptation to change, and the operationalization of these changes into daily activities, which in turn funds more innovation.

What does this look like through the lens of the Cynefin framework?

Chaotic problems are first stabilized (triage), and they evolve into complex problems that are analyzed, then they are broken down into manageable components, which may eventually lead to operational standards where they can perform at scale and generate profits, to fund further innovation. The evolutionary cycle shown in this illustration is the premise of my book "Run Grow Transform[14]" published in 2012.

---

[14]"Run Grow Transform: Integrating Business and Lean IT" by Steven Bell https://amzn.to/35hQgte

their way forward, and not – in the traditional management mindset – just "do the work, and do as they're told." In many developing countries, however, this authoritative leadership style is deeply embedded in the culture, and requires a great deal of sustained effort to overcome.

Once the team agrees on their target condition, they begin analyzing the problem using a variety of empirical techniques, formulating hypotheses, designing and conducting experiments to iteratively validate or disprove these hypotheses, and pivoting when new information is uncovered. This is the scientific method, the foundation of continuous improvement.

It is important to understand that all problems are not alike. A brief mention of the Cynefin decision making framework is useful here[12]. Problems can be Simple, Complicated, Complex and Chaotic.[13]

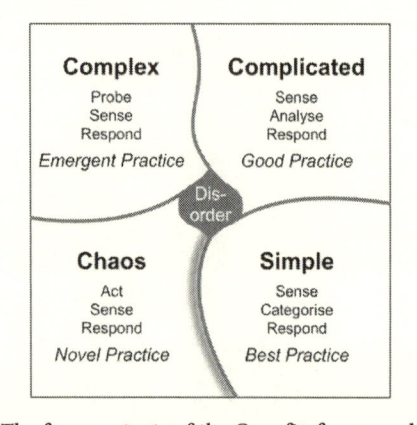

Complex	Complicated
Probe	Sense
Sense	Analyse
Respond	Respond
Emergent Practice	Good Practice

Dis-order

Chaos	Simple
Act	Sense
Sense	Categorise
Respond	Respond
Novel Practice	Best Practice

The four contexts of the Cynefin framework

Simple and complicated problems are deterministic, driven by precision and standards. Simple problems can be resolved through agreement and implementation of standard work, supported by

---

[12]Cynefin framework. Wikipedia https://en.wikipedia.org/wiki/Cynefin_framework

[13]"The Quality of a Design will not Exceed the Knowledge of its Designer; an Analysis Based on Axiomatic Information and the Cynefin Framework" - Scientific Figure on ResearchGate, image available from: https://www.researchgate.net/figure/The-four-contexts-of-the-Cynefin-framework-When-in-disorder-the-actual-context-is-not_fig2_283194976

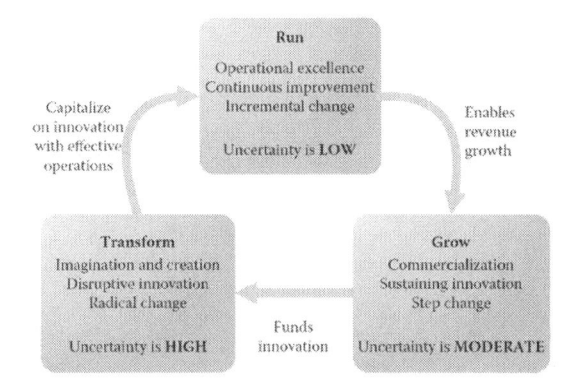

Steve Bell: Simple Framework for Complex Problems

```
                          Run
                  Operational excellence
                  Continuous improvement
     Capitalize      Incremental change      Enables
     on innovation                           revenue
     with effective  Uncertainty is LOW      growth
     operations

     Transform                               Grow
  Imagination and creation            Commercialization
   Disruptive innovation              Sustaining innovation
      Radical change                     Step change
                          Funds
   Uncertainty is HIGH   innovation   Uncertainty is MODERATE
```

From the book, 'Run Grow Transform: Integrating Business and Lean IT' by Steven Bell

For an ideal example of such evolution, look at the decades of innovation and operationalization of Apple Computer, and the dramatic effect they have had on the daily lives of a significant percentage of the worlds' population.

Living in the age of VUCA, every organization must learn how to adapt and thrive through continuous change. This is why problem solving across the full spectrum of problem-types is an essential skill for everyone in the organization. Lean, Six Sigma, and Agile (including the Scrum method) provide a variety of approaches to various types of problems. But for starters, it's helpful to understand the steps of the popular Lean problem solving method called A3[15]. It is a step-by-step playbook that can help any team, in any situation, begin to unravel a problem.

---

[15]"Managing to Learn: Using the A3 Management Process to Solve Problems, Gain Agreement, Mentor and Lead" by John Shook https://amzn.to/31Z3qcB

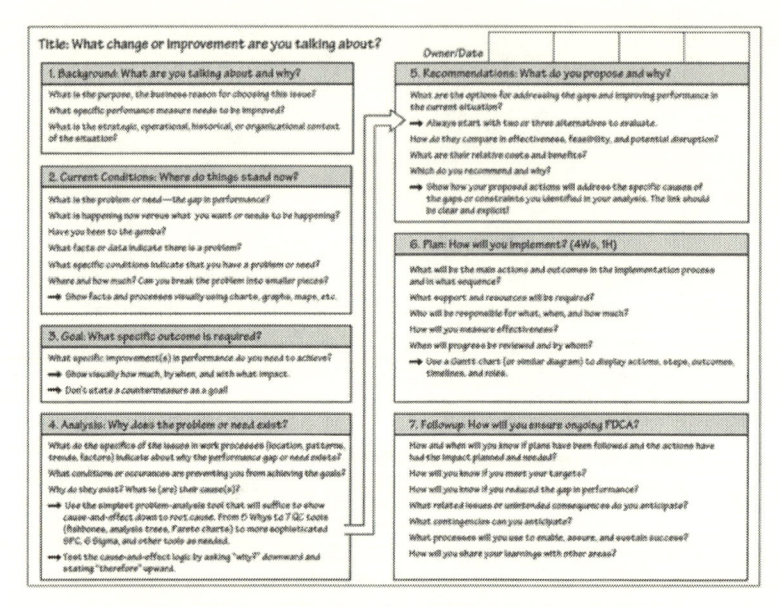

Detailed A3 Explanation from 'Learning to See' by John Shook

This careful, rigorous approach to problem solving does not come naturally to most people, and most organizations, so it must be actively taught and coached. I have found that even in today's sophisticated, data-driven world, many organizations have deep analytical capability (both humans and machines) for their overall approach to problem solving. However, how they best apply that plentiful data (using experiential evidence, and a broad, contextual perspective from multiple points of view across the organization) is often lacking. Organizations that are successful at developing this skill can empower people and teams to solve their own problems with autonomy, mastery and shared purpose to guide their own actions towards desired outcomes.

However, empowerment of teams with decision making skills alone is insufficient and can be dangerous. It's helpful to remember that Peter Senge (founder of the Society for Organizational Learning) emphasized that empowerment without alignment is chaos. Problems usually offer a variety of potential solutions, and can be analyzed from a variety of perspectives. A team must decide what outcome they are solving for, and what tradeoffs they are willing to make. Every team must have a clearly shared purpose so they can agree on where they're going. They must also have a gestalt view, a True North alignment to the overall enterprise, and clarity on how their localized efforts serve the larger enterprise, its customers and its evolving mission.

This leads us to the third aspect of Lean Thinking and continuous improvement, the role of leadership, management, and management systems. They serve to help everyone understand the direction the organization is going, to collectively align their compasses and synchronize their watches, continuously learning and adapting together as they move into an increasingly uncertain and volatile future.

The Learning Organization

Traditional management systems, historically taught in business schools and learned on the job, often involve top down, command and control mentality. This assumes leaders understand the problems and know what needs to be done. In an organization of any size and complexity, we have learned time and time again that this is usually not the case.

Each individual, whether a senior leader, a manager, or a frontline team member, must realize that the only way they can succeed is by harnessing the collective perspectives and ideas of everyone. To achieve this, leaders must create a culture of teamwork and problem solving. In the world of nonprofits and NGO's, this can mean establishing a clear and collective purpose and sense teamwork that crosses multiple organization, governmental and cultural boundaries. They strive to combine empowerment with alignment to help everyone learn, adapt, and move forward together, and quickly pivot when conditions change.

Lean practitioners have learned that simple visual management and communication can be very powerful in bringing teams and organizations together with a minimum of distraction, wasted meetings, and confusion. Effective visual management can help make demand, flow, problems and outcomes visible to all, at every layer of magnification, from top level strategic activity to frontline work.

This helps everyone, at every dimension of the organization, answer the questions:

- What problems must we focus on now?
  * Across the entire organization?
  * For our localized team?
- What have we done about these problems?
- What are the outcomes?
- What about our current working hypothesis did we validate and/or disprove?
- What have we learned after serious reflection and further analysis?
- What are we going to do next?

With effective visual management crossing dimensional boundaries, vertically from strategy to the frontlines, and horizontally across value streams, anyone, at any time, should be able to see and understand how all the pieces flow together, and quickly spot problems.

A smooth, regular cadence of collaboration (supported by effective visual management) helps to keep everyone moving together. Daily cascading team huddles (also often called 'standups') help everyone assess daily priorities and problems. Periodic 'catchball' sessions reconcile strategic goals with outcomes and lessons learned, helping each team solve the right problems (empowerment) with the right shared goals for everyone (alignment). There are fewer formal meetings, replaced by a continuous flow of information, communication and collaboration across the enterprise. When a sudden problem arises, the organization has the muscle memory to instantly swarm the right resources to it.

From this living, breathing, pulsing, neural-network-style organization emerges what is often called a "learning organization."

Lean and Six Sigma for humanity and the planet

Lean and Six Sigma practice have been evolving in large organizations for decades. They began in manufacturing, and have rapidly evolved across every industry. While workflow looks quite different in healthcare and financial services, it's easy to see how the underlying principles and practices are valid in all cases. There is no doubt that these practices can help with our present need to address chaotic environmental concerns, accelerating the development and efficient delivery of an alternative energy global infrastructure, while addressing a host of other complex issues.

As I emphasized at the start of this chapter, Lean and Six Sigma are not just for large companies and global problems. They are effective with small organizations, and even individuals, at a local level. For example, Lean thinking can be effective in supporting microenterprises in developing countries and communities around the world. One woman, with a small microloan, can make a substantial difference for her family and her community. These principles can help her gain useful guidance on how to keep focused, simple and efficient.

Microcredit and microenterprise was first popularized by Nobel peace prize laureate Muhammad Yunus, founder of Grameen Bank. They have become enormously effective tools for economic and community development, and their application has benefited from Lean thinking. Decades ago, as the founding secretary for Rotary International's Microcredit Action Group, I had the good fortune to witness it in action around the world. For more on this, see Douglas Cooper's chapter in this book about his work with Mercy Corps Northwest, and also a video "Reaching the last mile of poverty"[16] of our work with Grameen Foundation in Uganda.

Reaching the "Last Mile" of Poverty: Creating Value for the Poor with Lean IT

Khuloud Odeh   Steve Bell
Lean>NGO

Lean IT Summit
3 &4 October, 2013
Paris, France

GRAMEEN FOUNDATION
Connecting the World's Poor to Their Potential

Grameen Foundation presentation "Reaching the last mile of poverty" from Khuloud Odeh

The bottom line is this: every individual, team and organization, wherever they are, and whatever they are doing, can benefit from Lean thinking. They can use simple tools like visualizing flow, holding daily huddles around a kanban board covered with sticky notes, and a simple A3 problem solving storyboard.

This is why Karen Whitley Bell and I introduced Lean4NGO.org[17] in 2008. It is a free, internet-based community bringing Lean, Six Sigma and Agile practitioners together with NGOs and nonprofits around the world. It is our hope that every for-profit organization around the world with an internal Lean, Six Sigma or Agile coaching staff will engage in outreach to help develop those skills within the NGO and nonprofit community. By doing so, these for-profit organizations will further develop their own internal

---
[16] Reaching the last mile of poverty: Dr Khuloud Odeh, CIO of Grameen Foundation https://www.youtube.com/watch?v=FCzPRyXBej0

[17] Lean4NGO, an organization founded by Steve Bell and Karen Whitey Bell to incorporate Lean principles in support of mission-driven non-profits and NGOs, https://www.lean4ngo.org

coaching skills, experience and perspectives. It's a win-win-win.

Lean4NGO.org

As I said at the beginning, I'm grateful that Brion has released this new book. His tireless efforts to search out stories, encourage them to be recorded, to edit and publish them as case studies, is uniquely valuable and useful. As we learn from the stories of others, we can see how we might use these approaches in our own efforts to help make the world a better place for all.

Proceeds

The proceeds of this book chapter will be applied to ongoing costs such as website operation and development of Lean4NGO.org. Lean4NGO is presently self-funded and does not qualify to receive tax deductible donations. Note: any out of pocket costs such as travel and expenses to support our nonprofit clients are funded by each project and are not covered by proceeds from this chapter. Learn more at Lean4NGO.org.

Contact

Steve Bell is a master coach and pioneer of Lean IT and Lean Digitization. He is the author of Lean IT, Run Grow Transform, Lean Enterprise Systems, Accelerate, and numerous other published works. He is a two-time recipient of a Shingo award, in 2011 for Lean IT (Shingo Prize for Research and Professional Publication) and the 2019 (Shingo Publication Award) for Accelerate. Steve, and his partner Karen Whitley Bell, co-founded Digital Lean Strategies and Lean4NGO.

Email: steveb@digitalleanstrategies.com
LinkedIn: https://www.linkedin.com/in/leanITcoach
Website: https://www.digitalleanstrategies.com
Phone: 503-789-8627

Elisabeth Swan: Leaning into the Mission of Childcare

A nonprofit daycare center is about as far from manufacturing as you might imagine. Although many associate Lean Six Sigma with making widgets, Cape Cod Child Development ended up using classic process improvement techniques to expand their operations. They also learned, like many manufacturing plants before them, that lasting success depends upon the human element. The team hit intangible speed bumps while they sussed out what worked ... and how to learn from what didn't work.

Having travelled the world for over 30 years as a Lean Six Sigma Consultant, it was gratifying that one of my most satisfying experiences happened in my backyard. I got a call from the CEO of a local nonprofit near my home on Cape Cod, Massachusetts. Her work in the private sector exposed her to the benefits of becoming Green Belt certified in continuous improvement. She wanted that for her new leadership team, so we set out to make it happen.

The stories here are real, as are the charts and data. The choice to illustrate the graphs and forms is intended to make them more readable and relatable. Some illustrations simply capture the spirit of the team's journey. This group did amazing and admirable work.

Cape Cod Childcare Development ran Head Start programs, counseling for teen mothers, daycare centers, aid for the homeless, and many other efforts revolving around caring for children in need. The CEO applied for and received a grant to cover the cost of training and coaching the group. The next step was to get a return on the investment.

The project focus areas ran the gamut. One effort involved increasing the number of people who properly self-identified as homeless to get them the help they needed. Another focused on decreasing dangerous incidents in the daycare centers. Another sought to increase the amount of time-based "in-kind" donations from parents and community members. What turned out to have the biggest impact was an effort to reduce expenses.

That effort also ran up against the most resistance. Cutting expenses is what most people associate with efforts like Lean. They often interpret "LEAN" as referring to cutting people (Less Employees Are Needed) as opposed to removing wasteful activities to better serve customers. Business author Tom Peters said, "You can't shrink yourself to greatness." Yet shrinking expenses turned out to be something great.

The first step was to identify the process to address. "Expenses" are what we call a "bucket" since it's generally the result of multiple processes. The project lead, who was the office manager, wanted to focus primarily on the process of buying supplies. She witnessed daily the free-wheeling system involved in keeping the many facilities stocked and operational.

Process Walk Discoveries

The office manager took on the expense reduction project because it drove her crazy to see waste. As part of her Define Phase, she conducted a tour—a Process/Gemba Walk—of the properties. She found daycare centers with unused dishware and idle dishwashers, and teachers ordering paper plates, plastic utensils, and cups instead. Mapping out the process led her to describe the supply ordering system as "Buy As You Wish."

Instructors had access to company credit cards, so they ordered what they needed when they needed it. She knew they had the welfare of the children in mind, and her research turned up nothing out of the ordinary. No one was ordering Diamond Barbie Dollhouses or Louis Vuitton Teddy Bears. The supplies made sense. It's the process that lacked coherence.

Each person used their vendor of choice. They all ordered their own cleaning supplies, paper, crayons, books, construction blocks, or whatever they needed. They used local stores, made trips to Walmart, and ordered online. They picked up the items themselves, used UPS, or the Post Office. She was the "tail of the dog" sending packing slips and receipts to the Finance department so they could determine what to pay the credit card companies.

As she moved into the Measure Phase, she established her baseline. The expenses averaged around $2500 per month.

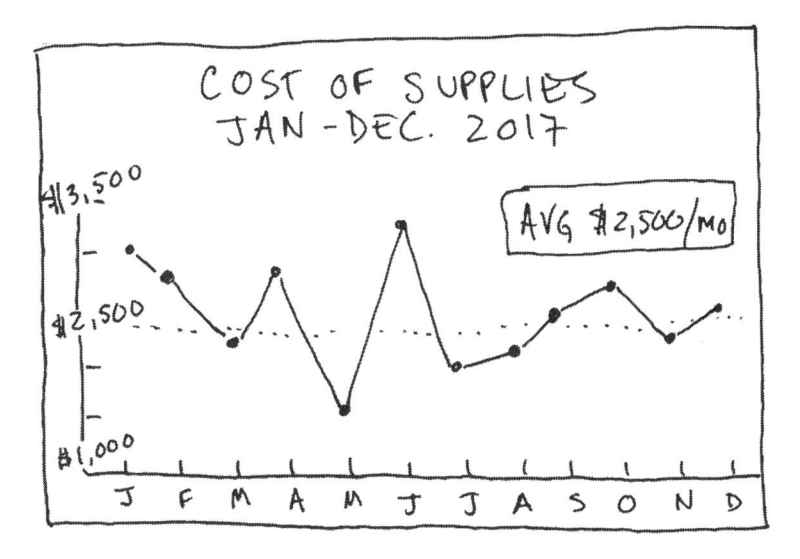

Figure 1: Time Chart of Cost of Supplies Baseline from Jan - Dec 2017

During the Analyze Phase, she'd learned a few things about ordering supplies for the organization's headquarters. She discovered there were vendors who offered discounts for bulk orders. She spoke to new contacts and discovered they had thresholds that allowed them to elevate clients into "preferred customer" status.

She dipped her toe into the Improve Phase to test out a cheaper all-purpose cleanser to potentially stock all the facilities. That seemed like a simple experiment. Not so fast.

The outcry over the new cleanser was swift and unhappy. Some rejected the smell, others found it irritating, and most asked, "why can't we use the cleaning supplies we want?" Similarly, when she suggested the daycare centers make use of their dishes and dishwashers, she was gently rebuffed. She was new, they'd been there a while, so she needed to rethink her approach. She returned to the data she'd collected.

She showed them the potential saving from running the dishwashers. She told them how cheaply she could order paper, crayons, or Legos. She offered to show them the charts and graphs she'd created, yet they were unmoved. The teachers reminded her they had systems that worked, and disrupting their efforts took time away from kids in need. She reached out for help.

She was new in her role as office manager, and she had zero

positional authority over the staff. Since she reported to the CEO, who was her project sponsor, she asked for her support in making changes to the ordering process. The CEO agreed that "Buy As You Wish" had run its course and it was time to consolidate vendors and make other changes as suggested. She was prepared to intervene where she was needed.

Wrestling with Resistance

As the office manager contemplated her next steps, she hesitated. Having the CEO fight her battle felt like a failure. It also raised the issue of her interactions becoming confrontational. She didn't want to engage with staff on that level. She wanted their support in her efforts. I let her in on a discovery I'd made during my years of coaching. Facts and data often fail to move hearts and minds. The next time we spoke she had shifted course.

One of the year's biggest organizational objectives was to purchase a facility to host an additional Head Start program. They subsisted on grants and there wasn't enough in the current operating budget to afford a new building, but there could be. She set her sights on reducing expenses enough to afford the monthly mortgage. She changed her message and sat down with administrators, instructors, and counselors. The impact was swift and exciting.

Improve Phase Revisited

Many staff members immediately approached her with cost-saving ideas. Some of them were tangential to the supply process. One colleague let her know she didn't need the cell phone she'd been given. She was using her own and hoped that by reducing the monthly fee, it could help with the effort to fund the new building. Once she began investigating the cellphone bills, she realized they were being charged for "ghost" phones that people were no longer using. That quick win by itself covered three quarters of the cost of a new mortgage.

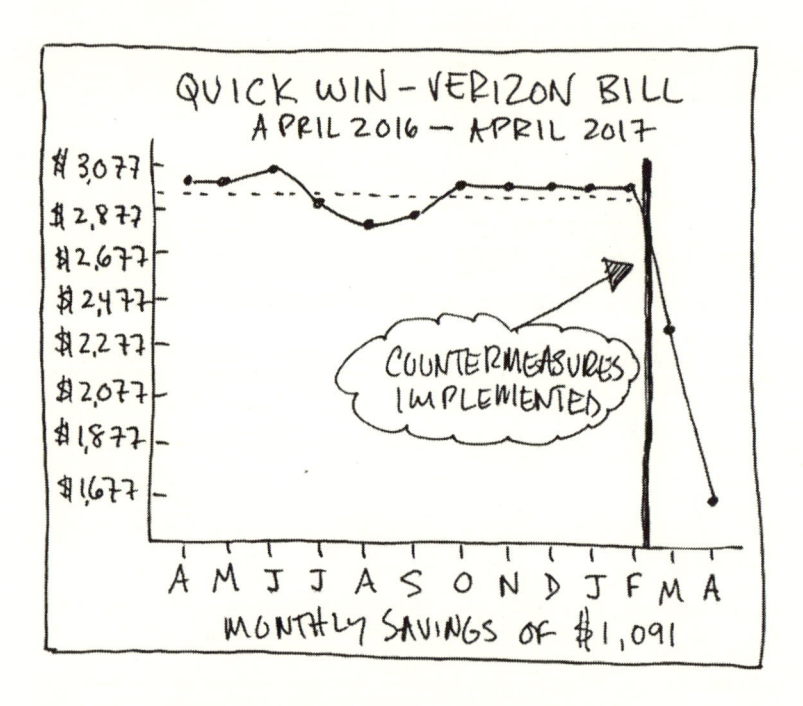

Figure 2: Time Chart of Before & After Verizon Bill

Listening to Stakeholders

She reflected on the staff's reaction to her experiment with new cleaning agents. She went back to her vendor of choice and asked for new options. She attended the next staff meeting with a sample of a different liquid cleanser to run it past them. She conducted a mini demonstration first by pouring the product on the table. It dissipated in 30 seconds with no residue. She rubbed the cleaner on face and hands to check for eye or skin irritation, and there was none. She let them know the product was used in Neonatal Intensive Care Units (NICUs). That is a hospital ward caring for the sickest babies. If it was safe enough for them, she offered, then it was what they needed for their sites. They were impressed with her efforts, and they were all in.

Expense Reduction Results

She managed to update the ordering process, consolidate vendors, reduce the number of steps involved in getting supplies to the people who needed them, all while ensuring the Finance Department received the right info to pay the bills. Removing the waste in the process created a satisfying backdrop to the savings achieved with the group's effort. The savings from the monthly cellphone bill, combined with switching to a new vendor, was enough to afford the mortgage for the building to house the new Head Start program.

New Year's Control Phase Party

The impact didn't end there. During that holiday season they were able to give out gift cards, and that January marked the first time in their nearly 50-year existence that the staff received raises. The savings continued. That one project gave them lots to celebrate. And there were many other projects with real benefits.

Helping the Homeless Project

Another member of the leadership team had responsibility for securing benefits and services for people in need. She was frustrated when candidates failed to accurately list themselves as homeless, since that meant they lost out on eligibility to enroll in the programs they needed most. She spoke to family advocates and people within the enrollment process. Her analysis led her to discover an opportunity within the application form itself.

The process required people to label themselves as "homeless" to get assistance. Many rejected that option because it carried a stigma of shame. When she arrived at the Improve Phase, she got permission to change the form. Instead of asking people to check the "homeless" box, she changed the wording to list an array of living situations. Options like "Live with Family" seemed to carry less baggage. That simple switch immediately doubled the number of people she was able to help.

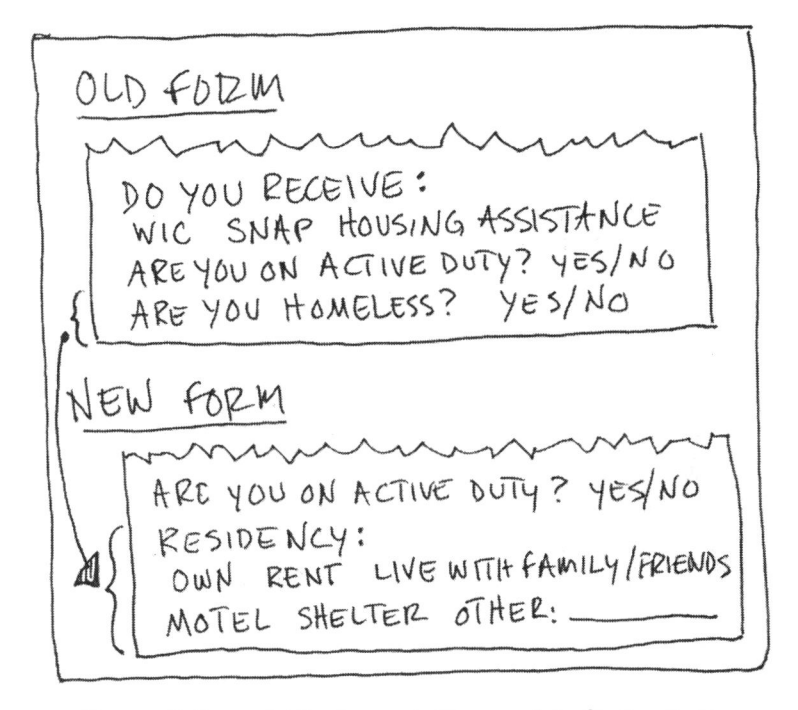

> **OLD FORM**
>
> DO YOU RECEIVE:
> WIC SNAP HOUSING ASSISTANCE
> ARE YOU ON ACTIVE DUTY? YES/NO
> ARE YOU HOMELESS? YES/NO
>
> **NEW FORM**
>
> ARE YOU ON ACTIVE DUTY? YES/NO
> RESIDENCY:
> OWN RENT LIVE WITH FAMILY/FRIENDS
> MOTEL SHELTER OTHER: _____

Figure 3: Before and After Segment of Improved Application Form

Reducing Incidents in Classrooms

Another member of the team oversaw the instructors of all the Head Start classrooms. She made it her goal to cut the number of classroom incidents in half. Incidents were defined as behavioral issues, accidents, property destruction, and emergencies within the classroom setting. During the Measure Phase, she found that teachers were submitting an average of 2 incident reports per classroom per day. That meant a median of 60 incidents per month. Incidents not only ran the risk of physical harm, but they also detracted from the children's ability to learn and grow. She needed to analyze the current state to better determine why the number of incidents were so high. Time to go to the source—where the incidents were happening.

Her Process/Gemba Walks involved spending time in each classroom. She watched the children interact with each other, their environment, and the teachers. What she observed was the impact of the room setup on the children. She saw children using shelving in the middle of the room as launch pads. She watched as other children tried to get out of the way of their more rambunctious classmates but had nowhere to go. It wasn't always clear where the areas to run ended and the places to read began. She realized there was an opportunity to rethink the space to drive better behavior.

During the Improve Phase, she worked with the teachers to reimagine the rooms. They removed the "launchpad" furniture from the center of the room. They created 2 separate "safe spaces" where children could retreat without being in the pathway of others. She also increased the open play area so children could express themselves more freely when they wanted to. They tested out the new room layout and experienced an immediate drop in incidents. But not all the data trended down.

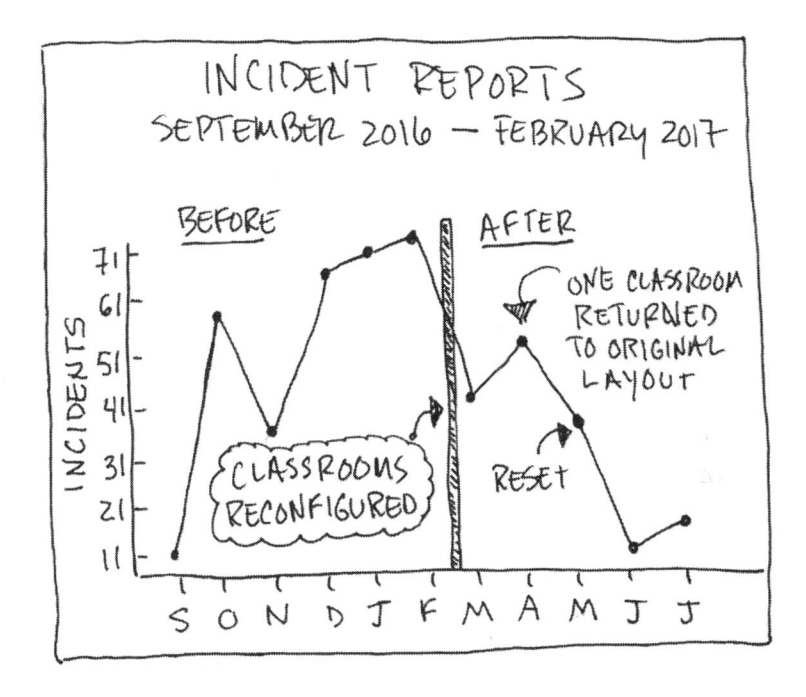

[Figure: Hand-drawn chart titled "INCIDENT REPORTS SEPTEMBER 2016 – FEBRUARY 2017" showing incidents over months S O N D J F M A M J J, with a "BEFORE" section peaking around 71, labeled "CLASSROOMS RECONFIGURED", then a "RESET" and "AFTER" section with "ONE CLASSROOM RETURNED TO ORIGINAL LAYOUT"]

Figure 4: Time Chart of Before & After Classroom Incidents from Sept 2016 - Feb 2017

The Hitch

There was one classroom where the incidents spiked back up. She was puzzled, so she visited the room. She discovered the teacher in that classroom had returned the room to the original layout over the weekend. When reflecting on why this happened, it turned out she hadn't had time to include this one teacher in the room redesign discussions. As a result, she had set this room up with the new design all by herself. She did it to save time, but it was a false economy. Realizing her mistake, she worked directly with the teacher to talk through the reasoning and the impacts. They reconfigured the room together. Problem solved.

Learnings

The improvements, gains, and returns on investment spanned every process, and the learnings were equally impressive. A sampling of a few key take-aways:

- Talk to everyone in the process—that includes the clients, the administrators, the management, and any stakeholders you can identify. You learn things like the negative impact of the word "homeless" and how to introduce words that work.
- Going it alone might be robbing someone of agency—the urge to do things yourself to save time and effort often leaves people feeling left out. You can avoid resistance to change—like the reconfiguration of a classroom—simply by including others.
- Charts and data often fail to move hearts and minds—it's key to consider the "why" of an effort. Once people understand your motives and goals—providing more facilities for children—they tend to become more emotionally invested.

Certified Problem Solvers

There were over a dozen projects with varying impact, and all positive. They saved money, reduced the time to hire, streamlined the grant process, and demonstrably improved their ability to care for children and other members of the community who needed them. For many, the process of collecting data, drawing process maps, constructing charts, conducting the 5 Whys, and using terms like "countermeasure" felt truly foreign. Initially many of them balked, but they showcased their work with pride.

They were also grateful that their Green Belt projects brought them closer to their colleagues in the field. Their work sparked conversations they'd never had. They discovered the advantages of not only asking better questions but listening to the answers. They prevailed, and they bonded as a leadership team.

Cape Cod Child Development Green Belt Class of 2017

Proceeds

Although they did vital work, and they did it well for decades (like many nonprofits), Cape Cod Childcare Development was dependent on grants to survive. After losing a major source of funding, they succumbed to bankruptcy in 2019. The loss of their programs and people are still rippling across vulnerable areas of the state. Based on the suggestions of several former staff, I will donate the proceeds from my chapter to Cape Cod Children's Place[18]. They are a local nonprofit with a similar mission, and they worked closely with Cape Cod Child Development over the years. Their mission is to advocate "for Cape and Islands future by building resilience, strengths and skills in children and families." There are always children who can use our help.

---

[18]https://capecodchildrensplace.com/

Contact

Elisabeth Swan has coaching, consulting, instructing, and guiding people in continuous improvement for over 30 years. She is a cohost of the monthly podcast "Just-in-Time Café" where she and Tracy O'Rourke interview Lean Six Sigma Leaders, review helpful apps, and field thought-provoking questions from the problem-solving community. She is co-author of "The Problem Solver's Toolkit: A Surprisingly Simple Guide to Your Lean Six Sigma Journey[19]," and author of the upcoming book, "Picture Yourself a Leader: Illustrated Microlessons in Navigating Change."

Email: ElisabethSwan@elisabethswan.com
LinkedIn: https://www.linkedin.com/in/elisabethswan/ [20]
Just-In-Time Cafe: https://www.jitcafe.com/ [21]

---

[19] https://bit.ly/3IH1497
[20] https://www.linkedin.com/in/elisabethswan/
[21] https://www.jitcafe.com/

Tracy O'Rourke: Increasing Meals Per Hour with Kitchens for Good

Authored by: Tracy O'Rourke, Sally Toister and Jennifer Gilmore

Kitchens for Good is exactly that, a place where kitchens do a lot of good. Founded in 2014, they are a 501(c)3 sustainability-oriented, nonprofit organization with food at the center of their mission.

The heartbeat of the organization is their tuition-free Apprenticeship Programs in Culinary, Baking, and Hospitality. The program helps people facing barriers to employment to gain the skills they need to create sustainable careers.

Their Apprenticeship Programs consist of approximately 3 months of technical and life-skills training, along with career coaching on their campus, followed by about 17 months of paid on-the-job training with one of their employer partners. In addition to acquiring dozens of requisite core competencies, apprentices practice environmental stewardship with root-to-stem/nose-to-tail (whole ingredient) cooking practices, reducing use of plastics, and composting.

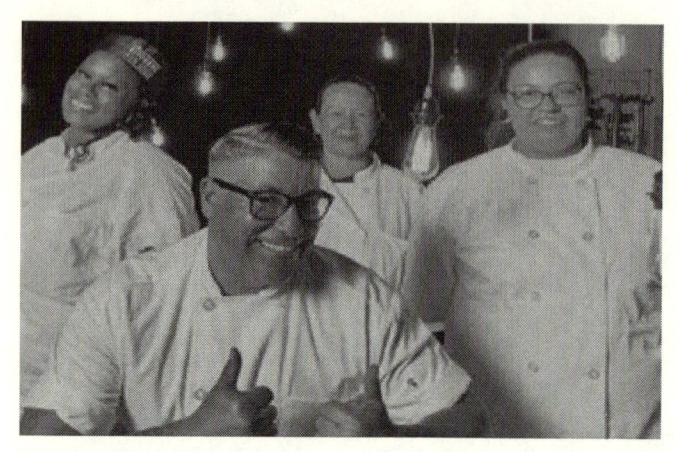

Chef students in the Culinary Apprentice Program at Kitchens for Good

Background

From 2019-2022, Kitchens for Good ran a hunger-relief program called Project Nourish, providing nutritious prepared meals to San Diegans. Project Nourish was able to combat hunger by preparing and distributing over 288,000 scratch-made, "Heat & Eat" meals annually throughout San Diego. Kitchens for Good fed people without access to affordable, nutritious food: children, seniors, and the unsheltered.

This initiative engaged Kitchens for Good culinary apprentices in daily opportunities to give back during their workforce training, often selecting people who had encountered hunger themselves. Kitchens for Good hunger-relief meals were distributed in partnership with other social services agencies including the San Diego Food Bank and their network of 500 social service agencies. This enabled them to distribute meals efficiently without duplicating distribution services.

Tracy O'Rourke: Increasing Meals Per Hour with Kitchens for Good 85

Left: Prepping meals for Project Nourish. Middle: Examples of the finished product before packaging. Right: A recipient enjoying a "Heat & Eat" meal from Kitchens for Good

As the program grew, Kitchens for Good struggled to efficiently achieve the higher packaging demand. To better service their community, the Operations leadership team enlisted the assistance of local Lean Six Sigma experts to partner with them to improve the process. Luckily, they were able to tap the talents of process improvement veterans Tracy O'Rourke, Sally Toister, Mike Osterling, and Marc Myers.

Sally Toister, Marc Myers, Mike Osterling, Tracy O'Rourke, and Lori Love onsite at Kitchens for Good with our masks during the Covid-19 Pandemic

The process improvement team arrived and set to work applying a classic process improvement approach to understand the problem and why it was happening, and then use their discoveries to make improvements. The first step was to clarify the presenting issue.

Problem Statement

Packaging meals took too long to meet demand. Meals were being packaged at a rate of 267 per hour, which was not fast enough to pack all the meals produced – with limited volunteer hours.

Once the team had clarified the problem, they worked with the Kitchens for Good staff to set the target.

Goal Statement

To achieve increased weekly production goals, meal packaging had to increase from 267 meals per hour to 560 meals per hour.

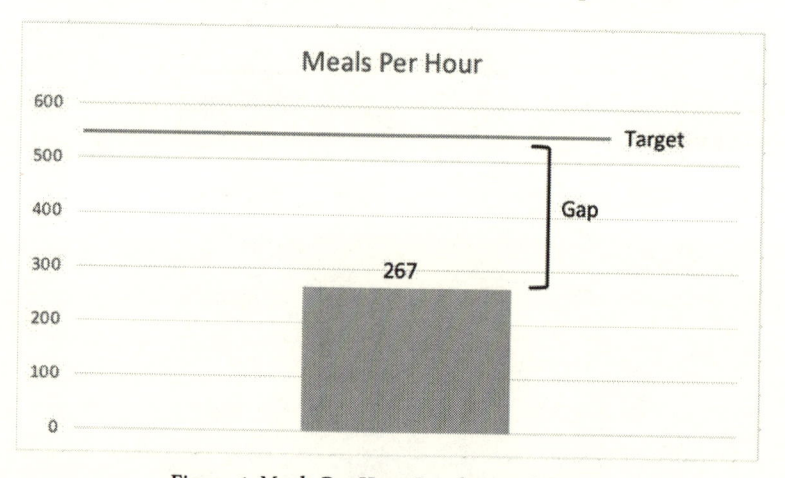

Figure 1: Meals Per Hour Baseline and Target

Current Condition

To better understand the current state, the process improvement team observed the process, interviewed the volunteers who worked in the process, and conducted some time and motion studies.

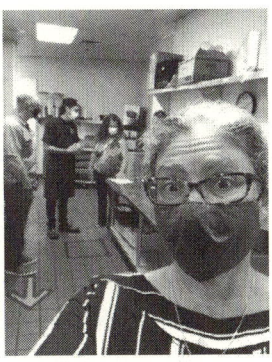

Left: The meal packaging area at Kitchens for Good. Right: The Consultants in the kitchen interviewing staff and volunteers about the process.

This enabled the Improvement Team to uncover some process root causes right away and they captured and organized them on a Fishbone Diagram. Pictured are some of the root causes discovered by observing the process and interviewing volunteers and staff:

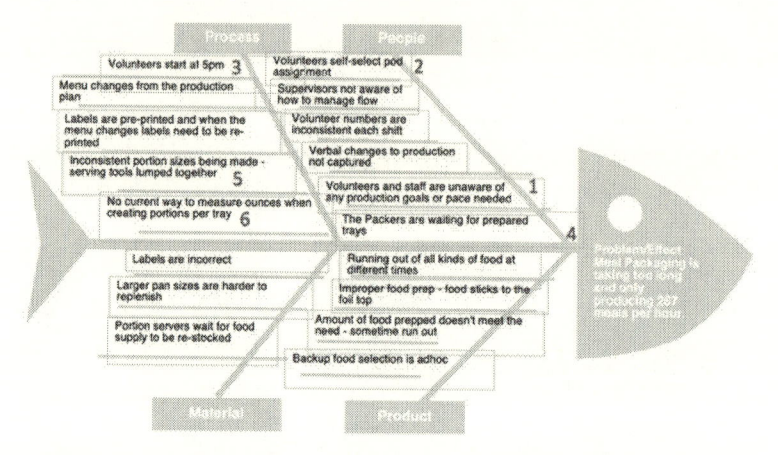

Figure 2: Fishbone Diagram of Potential Root Causes for Why Packaging Took Too Long

Below is a summary of the root causes the Improvement Team chose to address:

1. Volunteer and staff are unaware of any production goals or necessary pace.
2. Volunteers self-select pod assignments.
3. Volunteers start at 5pm.
4. The Packers are waiting for prepared trays.
5. Volunteers are creating inconsistent portion sizes and lumping serving tools together.
6. No current way to measure ounces when creating portions per tray.

Countermeasures Implemented for the Root Causes

Root Cause #1: Volunteers and staff are unaware of any production goals or necessary pace.

Solution: Establish a Takt Time and communicate the goal and production progress towards the goal.

The Improvement Team saw clearly that the process was not meeting Takt Time. Takt Time is the pace of customer demand, or how fast the process needs to run to meet the demand/goal. The formula is Net Available Work Time divided by Customer Demand. In this case, Kitchens for Good had 2 hours to make 1100 meals, which means the Takt Time was 6.54 seconds per meal.

The Improvement team decided to create 4 pods. Each pod would be assigned a certain number of meals. We took 1100 meals and divided them by 4 for a total of 275 meals per pod. The Takt time for each pod was 26.2 seconds per meal. We thought this might create anxiety for the volunteers, so to make it a little easier, we created a pitch of 35 meals every 15 minutes.

Sharing the production goal motivated the volunteers. They looked at the sheets and were curious about the data. They made it clear they wanted to help meet the goal. The Improvement Team was keenly focused on the process and making it better, as opposed to focusing on the people and trying to get them to work harder and faster.

For each pod, the Improvement Team created tracking sheets on flipcharts. They used these charts to track progress and capture any barriers to flow as production continued. Pictured are electronic reproductions of the flipchart tracking sheets.

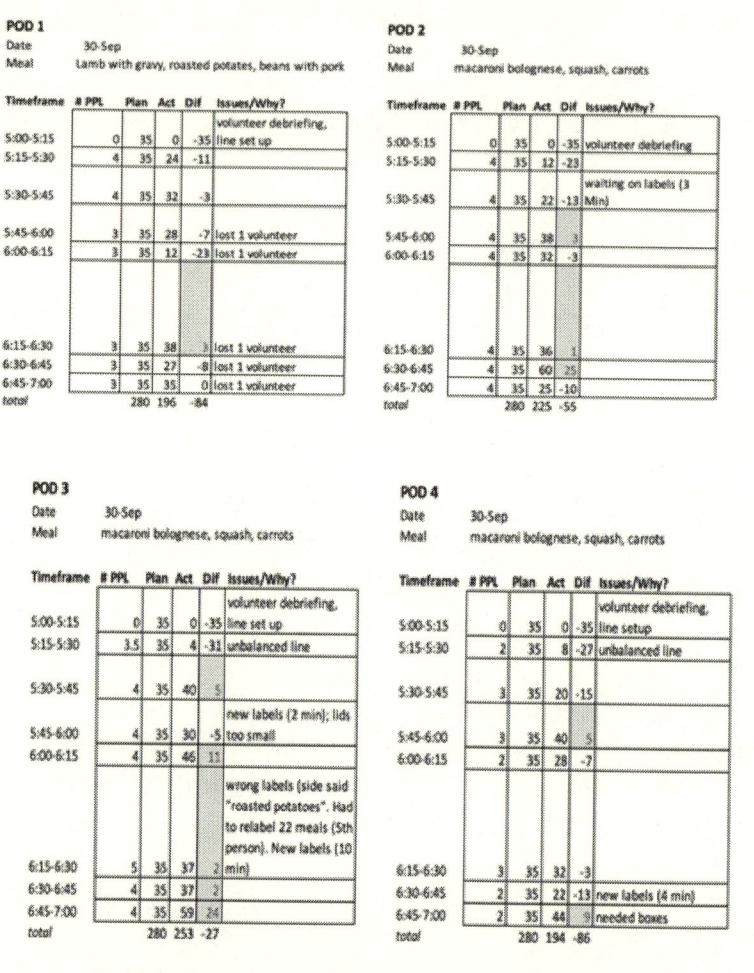

POD 1
Date: 30-Sep
Meal: Lamb with gravy, roasted potatoes, beans with pork

Timeframe	# PPL	Plan	Act	Dif	Issues/Why?
5:00-5:15	0	35	0	-35	volunteer debriefing, line set up
5:15-5:30	4	35	24	-11	
5:30-5:45	4	35	32	-3	
5:45-6:00	3	35	28	-7	lost 1 volunteer
6:00-6:15	3	35	12	-23	lost 1 volunteer
6:15-6:30	3	35	38	3	lost 1 volunteer
6:30-6:45	3	35	27	-8	lost 1 volunteer
6:45-7:00	3	35	35	0	lost 1 volunteer
total		280	196	-84	

POD 2
Date: 30-Sep
Meal: macaroni bolognese, squash, carrots

Timeframe	# PPL	Plan	Act	Dif	Issues/Why?
5:00-5:15	0	35	0	-35	volunteer debriefing
5:15-5:30	4	35	12	-23	
5:30-5:45	4	35	22	-13	waiting on labels (3 Min)
5:45-6:00	4	35	38	3	
6:00-6:15	4	35	32	-3	
6:15-6:30	4	35	36	1	
6:30-6:45	4	35	60	25	
6:45-7:00	4	35	25	-10	
total		280	225	-55	

POD 3
Date: 30-Sep
Meal: macaroni bolognese, squash, carrots

Timeframe	# PPL	Plan	Act	Dif	Issues/Why?
5:00-5:15	0	35	0	-35	volunteer debriefing, line set up
5:15-5:30	3.5	35	4	-31	unbalanced line
5:30-5:45	4	35	40	5	
5:45-6:00	4	35	30	-5	new labels (2 min); lids too small
6:00-6:15	4	35	46	11	
6:15-6:30	5	35	37	2	wrong labels (side said "roasted potatoes". Had to relabel 22 meals (5th person). New labels (10 min)
6:30-6:45	4	35	37	2	
6:45-7:00	4	35	59	24	
total		280	253	-27	

POD 4
Date: 30-Sep
Meal: macaroni bolognese, squash, carrots

Timeframe	# PPL	Plan	Act	Dif	Issues/Why?
5:00-5:15	0	35	0	-35	volunteer debriefing, line setup
5:15-5:30	2	35	8	-27	unbalanced line
5:30-5:45	3	35	20	-15	
5:45-6:00	3	35	40	5	
6:00-6:15	2	35	28	-7	
6:15-6:30	3	35	32	-3	
6:30-6:45	2	35	22	-13	new labels (4 min)
6:45-7:00	2	35	44	9	needed boxes
total		280	194	-86	

Figure 3: September 30th Pod Production Tracking Sheets

Root Causes #2 & 3: Volunteers start at 5pm and self-select their pod assignments.

Solution: Have volunteers come in earlier and assign pods to start up production as soon as possible.

If volunteers were restricted to showing up at 5pm or later, there was no chance to achieve the pitch of 35 meals in the 5:00-5:15

time frame. The choice was to either A) eliminate this time slot from production and recalculate Takt Time, or B) let the volunteers come in earlier so they could start the production line promptly at 5pm. The Kitchens for Good management team agreed to allow the volunteers to come in earlier (Option B).

The Improvement Team also observed that volunteers were allowed to walk the floor and randomly self-select which pod to join. This often led to a late production start, since low-staffed pods had to wait for other volunteers to show up before starting production.

The goal was to get production started as soon as possible. The solution allowed volunteer coordinators to assign volunteers to the pods to get production started right away.

Root Cause #4: The Packers are waiting for prepared trays.

Solution: Balance the line in the pod to minimize the waiting.

The original assignments were as follows:

- **Food Tray Filler**: This person would put the food portions for each food type into the tray.
- **Labeler**: This person would put a lid on the food tray and place a label listing all the ingredients on the lid.
- **Packer**: This person would take the finished product and put it in a box. Once the box was full, the packer would place the box as instructed, and get a new box to be filled.

The Meal Packaging Process. Left: Food Tray Filler. Middle and Right: The Labelers

The finished product before it gets distributed to the San Diego Community

During our time study, we gathered the following data:

Workload Balance vs. Takt Time

Takt Time = 26.2

Food Tray Filler · Labeler · Packer

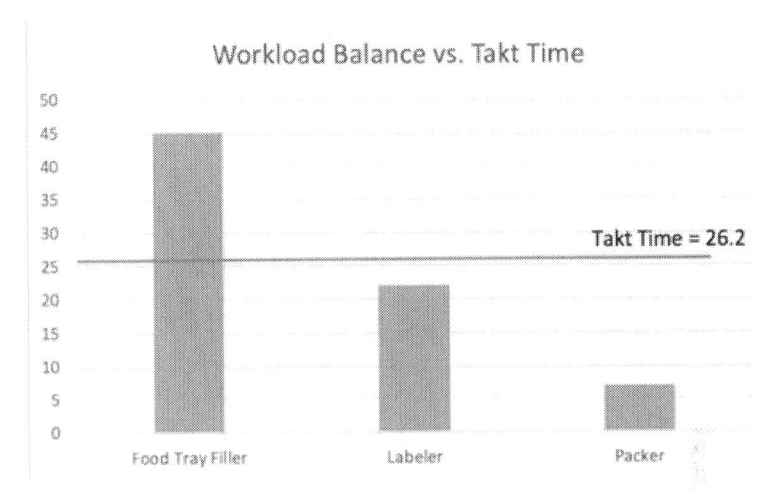

Figure 4: Percent Load Chart for Production Tasks

It was clear that the line was not balanced. The Food Tray Filler took much longer than the other tasks, and their task exceeded the target Takt Time. As Lean practitioners know, if any step exceeds the Takt Time, the process will not meet the Takt Time. The team had to address the imbalanced workload.

To meet the Takt Time, we transferred the Packer duties to the Labeler and reassigned that volunteer to become a 2nd Food Tray Filler.

We also moved the Packing process physically closer to the Labeling process to reduce the waste of motion, which shaved a few seconds off the Packers time.

Improved Workload Balance vs. Takt Time

Takt Time = 26.2

Food Tray Filler 1 | Food Tray Filler 2 | Labeler/Packer

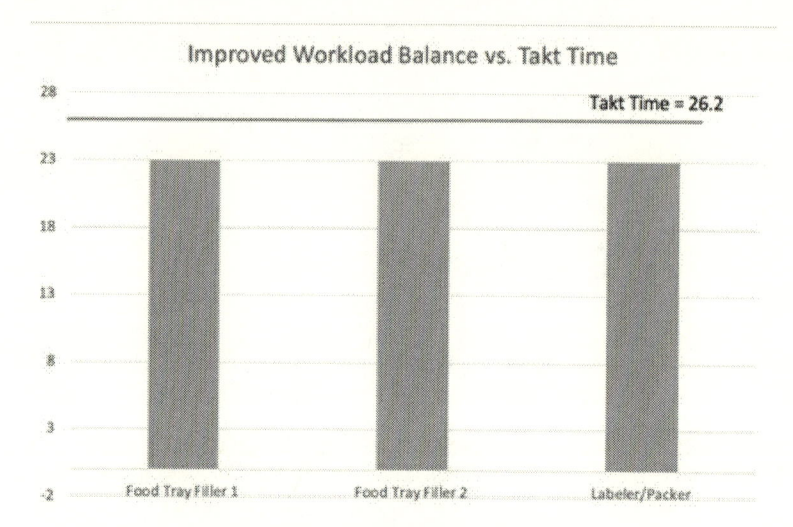

Figure 5: Improved Percent Load Chart

The Balanced Workload results were a clear improvement. The adjustments cut down on wait time and reduced the bottleneck for the Food Tray Filler. This really helped Kitchens for Good reach their target of 560 meals per hour.

Root Causes #5 & 6: Volunteers are creating inconsistent portion sizes and lumping serving tools together; No current way to measure ounces when creating portions per tray.

Solution: Create standard work for setup and portion sizes; add scales to each pod.

During the initial observation, many Kitchens for Good employees spent time correcting volunteers on appropriate portion sizes and pointing out which tools to use for each food type. This happened every evening and throughout the process since volunteers would come and go.

The process was repeatable, yet Kitchens for Good staff wasted a lot of time on volunteer oversight and manual correction. In addition, if errors were not caught early enough, there would be defects, errors and bottlenecks. The Improvement Team convinced the Kitchens for Good team that any time investment in developing standard work in this repeatable process would save them time later. They were all in.

The Improvement Team worked with Kitchens for Good staff to create standard work for the setup. This enabled early-arrival volunteers to help with all the prep. They also created better labels and clarified the exact tools to use for each food type at each station.

This minimized inconsistent portions and helped with the ever-present challenge of running out of food.

Left: The food being packaged and the corresponding ounces per tray. Middle: The utensils/tools to be used to portion the food correctly. Right: The total setup with the scales, utensils, and portion sizes.

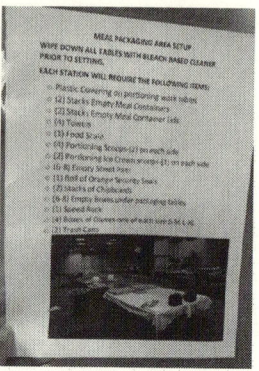

Left: The utensils in action with the bins. Right: The standard work for preparing the area for food packaging

After the initial efforts to improve the process, The Kitchens for Good staff continued to identify and implement solutions. The Improvement Team continued to check in with Kitchens for Good and help where needed.

After a few more weeks, they had additional improvements:

- Added carts to team stations for easier movement to boxing.
- Implemented flags to signal supply needs.
- Improved communication between the culinary and packaging teams.
- Adjusted food-serving bin size, making it easier and faster for volunteers to scoop food.
- Reduced non-value-added work from the packaging process.
- Simplified the process for volunteers.
- Reduced the motion of food.
- Reduced the overproduction of labels.
- Added visual management.
- Introduced nightly goal tracking.

Improvement Data

The collaborative effort achieved impressive results. Kitchens for Good and the Improvement Team improved meal production from their baseline of 267 meals per hour to their target of 560 per hour. Mission accomplished!

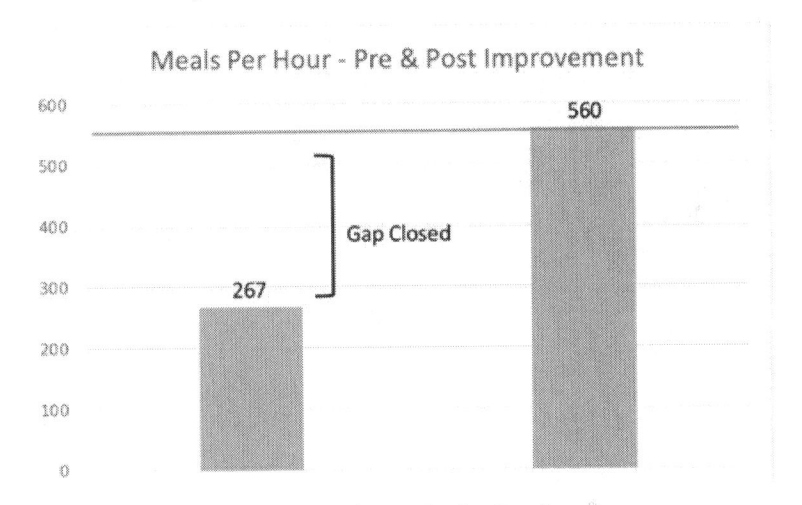

Figure 6: Before and After Results

After a few more weeks, Kitchens for Good managed to achieve 800 meals per hour! Project Nourish was able to reach thousands of people in need!

With the pandemic reducing in impact and the grant funds depleted, Kitchens for Good adjusted their strategy to focus once again on their core business, the tuition-free Apprentice Programs.

Kitchens for Good continues to leverage Lean Six Sigma Tools in other areas of the business.

In their new Kitchens for Good Retail Shop, they used process mapping and brainstorming tools to help design new processes and launch the grand opening. They managed to achieve their revenue targets in the first 90 days.

During some SalesForce application enhancements, the Kitchens for Good Team created operational definitions and developed a customer use analysis for a system upgrade to track the apprentice/partnership journey more effectively.

In the area of External Affairs, they built Swim Lane Maps to identify where to streamline the process to cultivate the Kitchens for Good donor base through repeat contributions.

Food packaging in the new Kitchens for Good facility

Packaging meals in the new Kitchens for Good facility

Kitchens For Good Volunteers and staff participating in Project Nourish

Below is the Executive Team at Kitchens for Good (January 2023).

Left to Right: Joanna Larson, Rachel Taylor, Natalia Moussa, Maggie McDermott, Brett Fisher, Lori Love, Juanita Atitsogbuie, and CEO Jennifer Gilmore.

Additional References

- Kitchens for Good: https://www.kitchensforgood.org [22]
- UC San Diego Process Palooza 2021 Spotlight Video [23]
- Local 10 News Project Nourish Spotlight Video [24]
- James Irvine 2020 Leadership Award Spotlight Video [25]
- New Kitchen Facility Local News Spotlight Video [26]
- Kitchens for Good - FY 2020-2021 Annual Report [27]

Proceeds

Proceeds for this book will be donated to Kitchens for Good[28]. Kitchens for Good produced and distributed 410,016 meals between March 2020 and March 2022. As restaurants began reopening, Kitchens for Good pivoted from disaster response to disaster recovery. This entailed transforming its meal prep kitchen into a teaching kitchen to help provide trained and motivated cooks, bakers, and food service managers to the recovering hospitality sector. Because of its contribution during Covid, Kitchens for Good was invited to serve as a member of the San Diego County Office of Emergency Services Feeding Taskforce and is currently participating in the development of a county-wide response plan to ensure equitable access to meals during times of critical need.

Contact

Tracy O'Rourke has been coaching, consulting, instructing, and guiding people in continuous improvement for over 25 years. She

---

[22] https://www.kitchensforgood.org
[23] https://www.youtube.com/watch?v=BbyGNcaBwDg
[24] https://www.10news.com/news/local-news/san-diego-news/grant-helps-san-diego-based-kitchens-for-good-expand-services-during-coronavirus-pandemic
[25] https://irvineawards.org/award-recipient/jennifer-gilmore/
[26] https://youtu.be/aMKhBOzRAXA
[27] https://kitchensforgood.org/wp-content/uploads/Annual-Report-2020-2021.pdf
[28] https://www.kitchensforgood.org

is a co-host of the monthly podcast "Just-in-Time Café"[29] where she and Elisabeth Swan interview Lean Six Sigma Leaders, review helpful apps, and field thought-provoking questions from the problem-solving community. She is co-author of "The Problem Solver's Toolkit: A Surprisingly Simple Guide to Your Lean Six Sigma Journey."[30]

Email: tracy@jitcafe.com
LinkedIn: https://www.linkedin.com/in/tracy-orourke/ [31]
Just-In-Time Cafe: https://www.jitcafe.com [32]

---

[29] https://www.jitcafe.com/
[30] https://bit.ly/3IH1497
[31] https://www.linkedin.com/in/tracy-orourke/
[32] https://www.jitcafe.com/

Joy Mason: Using Six Sigma to Address Racial Equity

My interest in process improvement goes back before I was even born. You could say it is in my genes.

My grandfather worked at Eli Lilly, a pharmaceutical company located in Indianapolis, Indiana. He worked during a time when almost everything was segregated between White and Black people, not only in the community, but also in the workplace. For the most part, there were only certain jobs that Black people could work, such as equipment maintenance or working with the animals.

Despite these barriers, my grandfather submitted a suggestion for how to make the feeding mechanism for the animals produce less wasted food. Animals would throw the food out of the cage and onto the floor, or it would get contaminated and would have to be thrown away (which costs the company money). His suggestion was to change the feeding process to salvage the food before it could be wasted or contaminated. It was so successful that he received a bonus in 1957 of $6,689, which was one of the largest bonuses given to an employee in company history at the time. It even made the local paper! The newspaper photo shows my mom and uncle around 10 or 12 years old at the time, and the picture is my family in front of their new house, which he bought using the bonus money as a down payment. Today, we would call his suggestion an example of continuous improvement.

As for me, I was born and raised in Indianapolis, and I went to college in Oxford, Ohio at Miami University. I always knew I wanted to go into the sciences, so I chose microbiology as my undergraduate degree. For one short moment, I considered art therapy but my family was not very supportive of that. When I graduated, I went straight to Eli Lilly and Company, following in my grandfather's footsteps.

I started in different roles like technical services and quality control, supporting commercial manufacturing. As my career progressed, I became a leader and manager over microbiological testing and environmental monitoring. During the last 10 years of my career, I worked on change management and project management for our international laboratories. That is when I became certified as a Six Sigma Black Belt. It was the most significant thing that I did for my career and for my life purpose. Since then, I've been applying my Six Sigma and continuous improvement skills to my work and to my community for good purposes.

In 2017, I retired from Eli Lilly after 30 years. But I wasn't done yet, as I saw the need for my skills in my local community. As a result, I founded Optimist Business Solutions[33], which is a training and consulting business that helps different firms, nonprofit and for-profit organizations to be more efficient and more effective. It has allowed me to leverage my skills in project management, change management, and continuous improvement to help these organizations. I started with nonprofit businesses, nonprofit agencies, and organizations that either were growing or weren't getting the outcomes that they were funded to achieve. I was able to help them with their processes, using tools like Value Stream Mapping (VSM) and Kaizen events.

What I would really like to share with you in this chapter is my work launching a nonprofit organization that uses Six Sigma methods to tackle Diversity, Equity and Inclusion (DEI) in Indianapolis.

---

[33] https://www.optimistindy.com/

Six Sigma Racial Equity Institute Logo

Addressing Racial Equity

In 2021 during the pandemic, I started to pivot more towards DEI programs. I knew I could apply the same change management, project management, and continuous improvement approach to help organizations achieve more tangible results from their efforts. What I could offer was different than what other DEI consulting firms were offering. They focused primarily on the soft skills and revisiting history. While that is meaningful and important work, it's hard to measure if this approach is impactful. When I spoke with other consultants, it appeared that they were not using a roadmap to measure progress.

In continuous improvement, we have tools like kaizen, Define Measure Analyze Improve Control (DMAIC) and Toyota Kata that guide us through tangible improvements in a structured way. With my background in Six Sigma, I prefer the DMAIC approach. My friend Deondra Wardelle prefers Toyota Kata for her Diversity and

Equity initiatives. The key is a focus on scientific thinking using data, teamwork and employee voices. DMAIC for DEI has become my unique value proposition.

After the murder of George Floyd, I was motivated and moved to create a nonprofit organization that would scale the DMAIC approach for equity, so I founded The Six Sigma Racial Equity Institute™. It is an innovative leadership program designed to upskill Black Women to be complex problem solvers. Participants in the program earn a Six Sigma Green Belt certification by completing training from a local university, and by completing an equity project in the local community.

Project sponsors come from many different sectors in the community, such as the superintendent of a school district or a leader over a homeless shelter for women. The project sponsors are excited about the program because they receive a team of driven and purpose-led women with a powerful new skill set and they do not have to pay for the team's assistance. The project sponsors get a team of 3 to 4 women that spend about 5 months working on an equity gap in their organization. The women in the program benefit because they earn their Green Belt certifications and practice their skills on a real-life important project.

My role is to raise money to get this program funded. Funding helps me create the infrastructure to allow these projects to happen. The primary goal is to upskill these women. The secondary goal, which is just as important, is to help organizations address equity gaps more effectively.

It's a win-win-win for everyone, which is why I'm so excited about this program!

The Importance of Data

What I like about the Six Sigma DMAIC framework is that you can tell if you're making progress because you're very clear about defining a problem statement. The focus on data provides a feedback loop that focuses you on what the data says, and helps ensure you are measuring the right thing. It also helps ensure that you're not spending time and money taking the team down the wrong direction.

I was in quality control for many years, so data was core to our work. We spent a lot of time on data integrity and data pedigree, especially in a regulated market like the pharmaceutical industry.

However, when working with other organizations (especially those that are nonregulated), in many cases there is a lack of understanding or focus on collecting data, along with how to analyze it to inform strategic decision-making. This approach challenges you to apply a data lens to equity when your organization doesn't necessarily have a strong data culture. This focus on data has become more evident in our second cohort. The first cohort was the pilot program and the participants identified their own projects. In the second cohort, I made some improvements by identifying five projects and working closely with the project sponsors. In 2023, I plan to spend even more time with the project sponsors, as it is so important for sponsors to understand the requirements for an impactful Six Sigma project.

Project Examples

When I started Optimist, I was fortunate to work on a project focused on homelessness. That project opened up some connections with the individuals and agencies who are in that space. This helped me identify a project that is focused on women and their children who are admitted into shelters because their families are experiencing homelessness. The team is looking at some equity issues between White families and Black families with respect to how long it takes to place Black women into housing. We were told that the Black families spend more time in the shelter than other ethnicities. When we dug into the Measure phase, we find that this was not true. Another reason why I like the DMAIC approach.

Another project we are working on is Free Application for Federal Student Aid (FAFSA). In the United States, you complete this form if you want to determine eligibility for financial aid and scholarships to help pay for college. The initial data shows that Black students and families do not complete the FAFSA form at the same rate as their White counterparts. Even though the application rate varies, the number of Black students completing the FAFSA exceeds other ethnicities.

Another project we're working on is supplier diversity. Oftentimes, large government agencies and entities contract with other large businesses as prime contractors to execute and complete internal projects. Black, female, and other minority organizations are typically subcontractors to the prime contractors because they're not big enough or have enough capital and resources to win those contracts.

Vicki Bonds (left) and Tamara Winfrey-Harris (right) work together on their Six Sigma project in Cohort 2.

When the entities take too long to pay their prime contractors due to inefficient processes, that can negatively impact prime contractors. The longer they take to pay, the longer it takes to pay the subcontractors, sometimes up to 90 days or later. These small businesses don't have the cash flow to cover expenses for up to 90 days from the time they provide the services until they get paid. The goal is to reduce how much time it takes for the entity to pay the prime contractor, and ultimately how long it takes to pay the subcontractor. The key is to find a solution that is within the control of the organization. There are some things that the entity can put in place from a process-perspective that can influence the prime contractors' payment process. Another key is to provide some incentives to move through progressive payments in a way that benefits everyone.

These examples represent just a few of the cohort's projects. While it may take some time to determine if the projects result in cost savings (like typical corporate Six Sigma projects), our primary focus is on closing equity gaps that impact Black people.

Advice for addressing equity

Did you know that we have over 150 cognitive biases[34]? Traditional approaches to addressing diversity and equity tend to focus on beating the biases out of you, but I don't think that's effective. One book I have read that shaped my views on this approach was "Diversity, Inc.: The Failed Promise of a Billion Dollar Business" by Pamela Newkirk.[35]

For organizations, the key is to focus on processes, not people. We're trying to get away from blaming people, but instead look at the systems and the processes first.

When we focus on the compensation process, the hiring process, the recruiting process or the promotion process, we shift away from symptoms and people's biases, which are harder to change. We get to the heart of the problem and implement strategies that will actually lead to better outcomes because the strategies target root causes.

After you have required your staff read antiracism books, formed your Employee Resource Groups (ERGs), and completed the basic diversity training, then I suggest focusing on improving a process that produces an inequity. It doesn't have to be a Six Sigma DMAIC project, but I love DMAIC because I think it's so intuitive. This helps tamp down some of the emotion that goes along with DEI work. If you look in our communities and our society, it's just very divided, it's very emotional, and it's very volatile. We need to find different

---
[34]https://gustdebacker.com/cognitive-biases/
[35]https://bit.ly/3XGwiBT

ways to bring people together to solve big problems to help make our communities better.

To summarize, our mission is to provide Six Sigma credentialing opportunities for Black people who are not given an opportunity for this type of certification, but also change the thinking and approach when it comes to diversity and equity. It seems to be working. We're approaching equity in a more innovative way that allows for more collaboration, while taking the volatility and emotion and blame out of the equation.

As I reflect on the Six Sigma projects that I had during my corporate career, these equity projects feel more meaningful. I'm not saying that my corporate projects weren't meaningful, but my Institute's projects are tackling very difficult community challenges while also providing more opportunities to upskill women. In summary, the work I did, the projects I had, the skills that I learned and the people I met over the past 30 years have led me here – founder of the Sigma Racial Equity Institute. I can't think of a better way to spend the tail end of my career than to do this truly purposeful work.

Proceeds

Proceeds received from my chapter will be donated to The Six Sigma Racial Equity Institute™[36], which is an innovative leadership program designed to upskill Black Women to be complex problem solvers through accredited Six Sigma Green Belt training and certification.

Website: https://www.sixsigmaindy.org/

Contact

Joy E. Mason is a Certified Six Sigma Black Belt with over 25 years of experience in pharmaceutical manufacturing, laboratory opera-

---

[36] https://www.sixsigmaindy.org/

tions, and risk assessment, with an emphasis on business processes and quality systems. Joy has managed international projects and effectively delivered results using six sigma methodologies for both public and private sectors.

As an internal consultant for a Fortune 200 company, Joy consistently created strategies and implementation plans to help clients meet new regulatory requirements. As an entrepreneur, Joy has helped clients dramatically improve their bottom line by applying her problem-solving techniques. Her strategies and techniques are proven to resolve process problems, evaluate risk, and save costs. She is known for her unwavering optimism and her unique ability to create a collaborative environment for diverse stakeholders to get things done.

Email: info@optimistindy.com
Website: https://www.optimistindy.com/
LinkedIn: https://www.linkedin.com/in/joy-e-mason-cssbb-06083722/[37]

---

[37] https://www.linkedin.com/in/joy-e-mason-cssbb-06083722/

Resources and Next Steps

Helping nonprofits

Would you like to volunteer your experience with a not-for-profit organization? You can search for volunteers groups near you (both US and International), and get advice on setting up your own volunteer group at the following website: http://www.leansixsigmaforgood.com/local-lean-six-sigma-and-nonprofit-groups/

Volunteer from Lean Portland help map the donation receiving floor layout at the Gresham (OR) ReStore.

Sharing your experiences

If you know someone who has spent time helping nonprofits or not-for-profit organizations apply process improvement techniques, please contact me at brion@biz-pi.com for more information about contributing to Volume 3.

Resources and Next Steps

Learn more

If you'd like to search for more case studies and examples of Lean and Six Sigma applied to nonprofits in different countries and different types of organizations, or to connect with our social media and networking platforms, please visit https://LeanSixSigmaforGood.com.

Made in the USA
Columbia, SC
21 February 2023